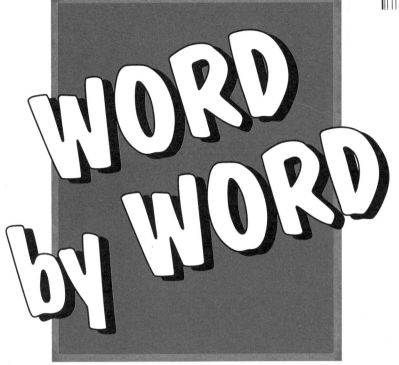

WORD by WORD

Картинный словарь английского языка

English/Russian Picture Dictionary

Steven J. Molinsky · Bill Bliss

Gennadi G. Gorbatov

PRENTICE HALL REGENTS, Upper Saddle River, New Jersey 07458

Publisher: *Tina B. Carver*
Managing editor, production: *Dominick Mosco*
Electronic production: *Tunde A. Dewey*
Interior design: *Kenny Beck*
Cover supervisor: *Marianne Frasco*
Cover design: *Merle Krumper*
Buyer/scheduler: *Ray Keating*

Illustrated by RICHARD E. HILL

In memory of our friend and mentor, Alex Lipson.

– Steve and Bill

© 1996 by Prentice Hall Regents
A division of Simon & Schuster
A Viacom Company
Upper Saddle River, New Jersey 07458

Printed in the United States of America

10   9   8   7   6   5   4   3

ISBN 0-13-125857-5

Prentice-Hall International (UK) Limited, *London*
Prentice-Hall of Australia Pty. Limited, *Sydney*
Prentice-Hall Canada Inc., *Toronto*
Prentice-Hall Hispanoamericana, S. A., *Mexico*
Prentice-Hall of India Private Limited, *New Delhi*
Prentice-Hall of Japan, Inc., *Tokyo*
Simon & Schuster Asia Pte. Ltd., *Singapore*
Editora Prentice-Hall do Brasil, Ltda., *Rio de Janeiro*

СОДЕРЖАНИЕ

ПРЕДИСЛОВИЕ

Картинный Словарь *Word by Word* содержит более 3,000 словарных единиц, представленных в живых, красочных картинках. Этот новаторский Картинный Словарь предлагает студентам необходимый словарный запас для эффективного общения в различных ситуациях и контекстах.

Словарные единицы в *Word by Word* разделены на 100 тематических разделов. Это даёт возможность организовать уроки в тщательной последовательности, начиная с непосредственного мира студента и кончая миром в широком смысле этого слова. Начальные тематические разделы, семья, дом и повседневные виды деятельности, ведут к урокам, посвящённым обществу, школе, работе, покупкам, отдыху и другим темам. *Word by Word* широко освещает важные виды деятельности, а также включает словарные единицы, посвящённые школьным предметам и внеклассным занятиям. Так как каждый тематический раздел в *Word by Word* представляет собой самостоятельную единицу, тематические разделы словаря могут быть использованы как в последовательности, представленной в словаре, так и в любом другом порядке.

Для удобства читателей, перечень тематических разделов в *Word by Word* представлен дважды: в последовательном порядке в Содержании, и в алфавитном порядке в Тематическом Индексе. Это, вместе с Глоссарием, представленном в приложении, даёт возможность студентам и преподавателям быстро и легко найти любое слово или тему в Картинном Словаре.

Картинный Словарь *Word by Word* занимает центральное место в целостной *Word by Word* Программе по Развитию Словарного Запаса, которая предлагает широкий набор печатных и наглядных материлов для преподавания на всех уровнях. Дополнительные материалы включают Рабочии Книги для трёх уровней (Элементарный, Начальный и Промежуточный), Книги для Учителя, Учебник по Методике Преподавания Словарных Единиц, Полный Комплект звуковых кассет, Настенные Карты, Цветные Диапозитивы, Игровые Карточки, Песенный Альбом и дополняющая его Книга Песен, а также Программа для Тестирования. Вы также можете приобрести Двуязычные Издания Картинного Словаря.

Методика Преподавания.

Словарные единицы в *Word by Word* представлены в контексте. В примерах диалогов показаны ситуации, в которых эти словарные единицы используются для непосредственного, значимого общения между людьми. Эти примеры являются основой вовлечения студентов в динамичную непосредственную разговорную практику. В дополнение к этому, в процессе обмена информацией о себе, своей культуре и странах, студенты имеют возможность с помощью письменных вопросов и вопросов для обсуждения, представленных в каждом разделе, установить связь между словарными единицами, темами и их жизнью. Таким образом, студенты могут познакомиться друг с другом "слово по слову."

При использовании *Word by Word* мы рекомендуем вам развивать методику преподавания, которая совместима с вашим стилем преподавания и нуждами и способностями ваших студентов. Надеемся,что для вас будет полезно познакомиться с методикой введения и практики словарных единиц в каждом разделе.

1. *Предварительный просмотр слов.* С помощью Настенной Карты, диапозитива, иллюстрации в *Word by Word*, или путём обсуждения, или написания слов на доске помогите студентам опознать слова, с которыми они уже знакомы.

2. *Введение Слов.* Укажите на картинку каждого слова, произнесите это слово и попросите класс повторить это слово хором или индивидуально. Проверьте понимание студентами этих слов, а также правильность их произношения.

3. *Практика Слов.* Попросите студентов работать над словами целым классом, в парах или в маленьких группах. Произнесите или напишите слово и попросите студентов указать на картинку этого слова, или сказать номер этого предмета. Или, вы можете указать на предмет или сказать номер, и попросить студентов произнести это слово.

4. *Разговорная практика моделей.* Некоторые разделы включают примеры диалогов, в которых надо использовать начальное слово из списка слов. Другие примеры представлены в форме скелетных диалогов, в которых можно вставить слова. (Во многих скелетных диалогах номера в скобках указывают на то, какие слова могут быть использованы для практики данного диалога. Если нет номеров в скобках, то можно использовать любое слово на данной странице.)

Следующие методические рекомендации могут быть предложены для Разговорной практики моделей:

а. Предварительный просмотр. Студенты смотрят на пример и обсуждают, кто, по их мнению, говорящие, и где происходит этот диалог.

б. Учитель знакомит студентов с моделью и проверяет их понимание слов, и того, что происходит в диалоге.

в. Студенты повторяют каждую строчку диалога хором или индивидуально.

г. Студенты практикуют модель в парах

д. Двое стедентов представляют новый диалог по примеру модели, при этом используя новое слово из данного списка слов.

е. В парах, студенты составляют новые диалоги по примеру модели, используя различные слова.

ж. Пары представляют свои диалоги классу.

5. *Дополнительная Разговорная Практика.* Во многих разделах даны два дополнительных скелетных диалога для дополнительной разговорной работы над словами. (Эти диалоги - жёлтого цвета в конце страницы.) Попросите студентов работать над диалогами и после, представить диалоги классу, при этом используя любые слова, которые они пожелают.

6. *Правописание слов и произнесение слов по буквам.* Попросите студентов работать над орфографией слов классом, в парах или в маленьких группах. Произнесите слово или произнесите слово по буквам, и попросите студентов написить это слово, а затем укажите на картинку этого предмета или дайте номер этого предмета. Или, укажите на картинку предмета или дайте номер, и попросите студентов написать это слово.

7. *Темы для Обсуждения, Сочинения, Журнальных записей и Папок.* Каждый раздел в *Word by Word* содержит, по крайней мере, один вопрос для дискуссии и сочинения. (Эти вопросы можно найти в конце каждой страницы зелёного цвета.) Попросите студентов ответить на вопросы классом, в парах или в небольших группах. Или, попросите студентов написать ответы дома, поделиться с другими студентами о том, что они написали, и обсудите всё это всем классом, в парах или в небольших группах.

Возможно, что студенты изъявят желание вести журнал относительно своих письменных заданий. Если позволит время, вы можете написать ответы в журналах ваших студентов, делясь с ними вашим опытом и мнениями, а также реагируя на то, что написали студенты. Необходимо отметить, что хранение сочинений в папках может помочь вам в оценке прогресса ваших студентов в изучении английского языка.

8. *Разговорные Виды Деятельности.* В Книге для Учителя в *Word by Word* представлен широкий выбор всевозможных игр, заданий, вопросов для дискуссий и других видов деятельности, цель которых максимально и эффективно использовать способности и возможности студентов. Для каждого раздела вы можете выбрать один или несколько видов активности, чтобы не только помочь студентам в освоении новых слов, но и сделать этот процесс стимулирующим, творческим, доставляющим удовольствие видом деятельности.

Цель Картинного Словаря *Word by Word* — предложить студентам разговорный, значимый и живой способ изучения слов английского языка. Мы надеемся, что, осветив суть нашей программы, мы также смогли передать и дух словаря: изучение слов может быть коммуникативным... релевантным к жизни студентов... отвечающим различным возможностям и способностям студентов... забавным и доставляющим удовольствие!

Стивен Молинский
Билл Блисс

The *Word by Word* Picture Dictionary presents more than 3,000 vocabulary words through lively full-color illustrations. This innovative Picture Dictionary offers students the essential vocabulary they need to communicate effectively in a wide range of relevant situations and contexts.

Word by Word organizes the vocabulary into 100 thematic units, providing a careful sequence of lessons that range from the immediate world of the student to the world at large. Early units on the family, the home, and daily activities lead to lessons on the community, school, workplace, shopping, recreation, and other topics. *Word by Word* offers extensive coverage of important lifeskill competencies and the vocabulary of school subjects and extracurricular activities. Since each unit is self-contained, *Word by Word* can be used either sequentially or in any desired order.

For users' convenience, the units in *Word by Word* are listed two ways: sequentially in the Table of Contents, and alphabetically in the Thematic Index. These resources, combined with the Glossary in the appendix, allow students and teachers to quickly and easily locate all words and topics in the Picture Dictionary.

The *Word by Word* Picture Dictionary is the centerpiece of the complete *Word by Word* Vocabulary Development Program, which offers a wide selection of print and media support materials for instruction at all levels. Ancillary materials include Workbooks at three different levels (Literacy, Beginning, and Intermediate), a Teacher's Resource Book, a Handbook of Vocabulary Teaching Strategies, a complete Audio Program, Wall Charts, Color Transparencies, Vocabulary Game Cards, a Song Album and accompanying Song Book, and a Testing Program. Bilingual editions of the Picture Dictionary are also available.

Teaching Strategies

Word by Word presents vocabulary words in context. Model conversations depict situations in which people use the words in meaningful communication. These models become the basis for students to engage in dynamic, interactive conversational practice. In addition, writing and discussion questions in each unit encourage students to relate the vocabulary and themes to their own lives as they share experiences, thoughts, opinions, and information about themselves, their cultures, and their countries. In this way, students get to know each other "word by word."

In using *Word by Word*, we encourage you to develop approaches and strategies that are compatible with your own teaching style and the needs and abilities of your students. You may find it helpful to incorporate some of the following techniques for presenting and practicing the vocabulary in each unit.

1. *Previewing the Vocabulary:* Activate students' prior knowledge of the vocabulary either by brainstorming with students the words in the unit they already know and writing them on the board, or by having students look at the Wall Chart, the transparency, or the illustration in *Word by Word* and identify the words they are familiar with.

2. *Presenting the Vocabulary:* Point to the picture of each word, say the word, and have the class repeat it chorally and individually. Check students' understanding and pronunciation of the vocabulary.

3. *Vocabulary Practice:* Have students practice the vocabulary as a class, in pairs, or in small groups. Say or write a word, and have students point to the item or tell the number. Or, point to an item or give the number, and have students say the word.

4. *Model Conversation Practice:* Some units have model conversations that use the first word in the vocabulary list. Other models

are in the form of *skeletal dialogs*, in which vocabulary words can be inserted. (In many skeletal dialogs, bracketed numbers indicate which words can be used to practice the conversation. If no bracketed numbers appear, all the words on the page can be used.)

The following steps are recommended for Model Conversation Practice:

a. Preview: Students look at the model illustration and discuss who they think the speakers are and where the conversation takes place.

b. The teacher presents the model and checks students' understanding of the situation and the vocabulary.

c. Students repeat each line of the conversation chorally or individually.

d. Students practice the model in pairs.

e. A pair of students presents a new conversation based on the model, but using a different word from the vocabulary list.

f. In pairs, students practice several new conversations based on the model, using different vocabulary words.

g. Pairs present their conversations to the class.

5. *Additional Conversation Practice:* Many units provide two additional skeletal dialogs for further conversation practice with the vocabulary. (These can be found in a yellow-shaded area at the bottom of the page.) Have students practice and present these conversations using any words they wish.

6. *Writing and Spelling Practice:* Have students practice spelling the words as a class, in pairs, or in small groups. Say or spell a word, and have students write it and then point to the picture of the item or tell the number. Or, point to a picture of an item or give the number, and have students write the word.

7. *Themes for Discussion, Composition, Journals, and Portfolios:* Each unit of *Word by Word* provides one or more questions for discussion and composition. (These can be found in a green-shaded area at the bottom of the page.) Have students respond to the questions as a class, in pairs, or in small groups. Or, have students write their responses at home, share their written work with other students, and discuss as a class, in pairs, or in small groups.

Students may enjoy keeping a journal of their written work. If time permits, you may want to write a response in each student's journal, sharing your own opinions and experiences as well as reacting to what the student has written. If you are keeping portfolios of students' work, these compositions serve as excellent examples of students' progress in learning English.

8. *Communication Activities:* The *Word by Word* Teacher's Resource Book provides a wealth of games, tasks, brainstorming, discussion, movement, drawing, miming, role-playing, and other activities designed to take advantage of students' different learning styles and particular abilities and strengths. For each unit, choose one or more of these activities to reinforce students' vocabulary learning in a way that is stimulating, creative, and enjoyable.

Word by Word aims to offer students a communicative, meaningful, and lively way of practicing English vocabulary. In conveying to you the substance of our program, we hope that we have also conveyed the spirit: that learning vocabulary can be genuinely interactive … relevant to our students' lives … responsive to students' differing strengths and learning styles … and fun!

Steven J. Molinsky
Bill Bliss

ЛИЧНАЯ ИНФОРМАЦИЯ

A. What's your **name**?
B. *Nancy Ann Peterson.*

имя	**1.** name		номер квартиры	**8.** apartment number
имя	**2.** first name		город	**9.** city
отчество	**3.** middle name		штат	**10.** state
фамилия	**4.** last name/family name/ surname		почтовый индекс	**11.** zip code
адрес	**5.** address		(региональный) код	**12.** area code
номер улицы	**6.** street number		номер телефона	**13.** telephone number/ phone number
улица	**7.** street		номер социального обеспечения	**14.** social security number

A. What's your _____?
B. ....
A. Did you say ....?
B. Yes. That's right.

A. What's your last name?
B. ....
A. How do you spell that?
B. ....

Tell about yourself:
   My name is ....
   My address is ....
   My telephone number is ....
Now interview a friend.

A. Who is she?
B. She's my **wife**.
A. What's her name?
B. Her name is *Betty*.

A. Who is he?
B. He's my **husband**.
A. What's his name?
B. His name is *Fred*.

жена	**1.** wife		брат	**8.** brother
муж	**2.** husband		ребёнок	**9.** baby

родители	**parents**		дедушка и бабушка	**grandparents**
мать	**3.** mother		бабушка	**10.** grandmother
отец	**4.** father		дедушка	**11.** grandfather

дети	**children**		внук и внучка	**grandchildren**
дочь	**5.** daughter		внучка	**12.** granddaughter
сын	**6.** son		внук	**13.** grandson
сестра	**7.** sister			

A. I'd like to introduce my _____.
B. Nice to meet you.
C. Nice to meet you, too.

A. What's your _____'s name?
B. His/Her name is ....

Tell about your family.
Talk about photos of family members.

ЧЛЕНЫ СЕМЬИ II

A. Who is she?
B. She's my **aunt**.
A. What's her name?
B. Her name is *Linda*.

A. Who is he?
B. He's my **uncle**.
A. What's his name?
B. His name is *Jack*.

тётя	**1.** aunt	тёща/свекровь	**6.** mother-in-law
дядя	**2.** uncle	тесть/свёкор	**7.** father-in-law
племянница	**3.** niece	зять	**8.** son-in-law
племянник	**4.** nephew	невестка/сноха	**9.** daughter-in-law
двоюродный брат/кузен	**5.** cousin	зять/шурин/деверь/свояк	**10.** brother-in-law
двоюродная сестра/кузина		невестка/золовка/свояченица	**11.** sister-in-law

A. Is he/she your _____?
B. No. He's/She's my _____.
A. Oh. What's his/her name?
B. ....

A. Let me introduce my _____.
B. I'm glad to meet you.
C. Nice meeting you, too.

Tell about your relatives:
   What are their names?
   Where do they live?
Draw your family tree and talk
   about it.

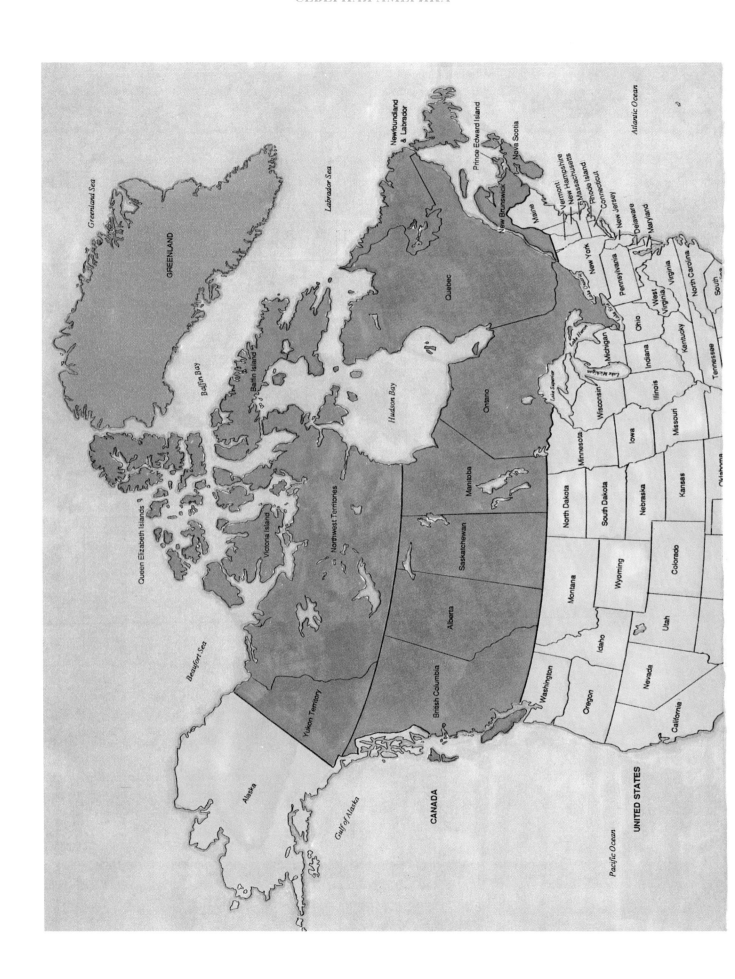

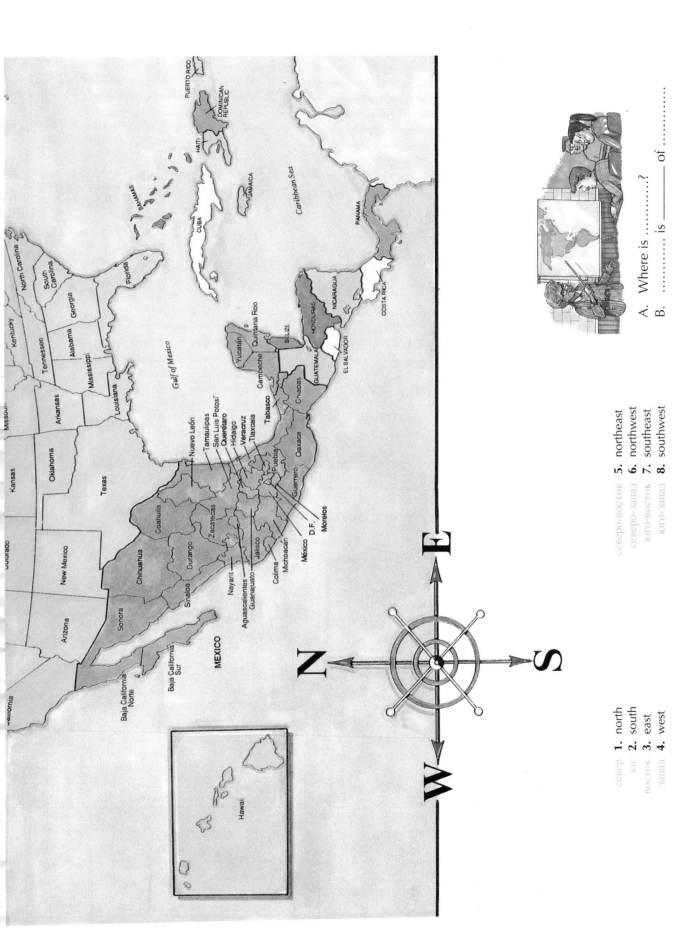

A. Where is ....?
B. .... is ____ of ....

север **1.** north
юг **2.** south
восток **3.** east
запад **4.** west

северо-восток **5.** northeast
северо-запад **6.** northwest
юго-восток **7.** southeast
юго-запад **8.** southwest

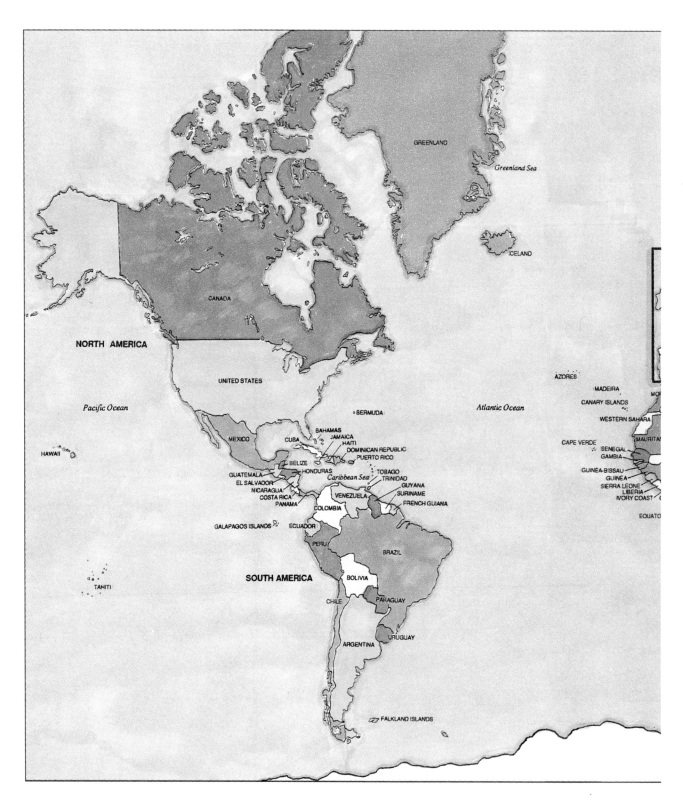

Северная Америка	**1.** North America		Ближний Восток	**5.** The Middle East
Южная Америка	**2.** South America		Азия	**6.** Asia
Европа	**3.** Europe		Австралия	**7.** Australia
Африка	**4.** Africa		Антарктика	**8.** Antarctica

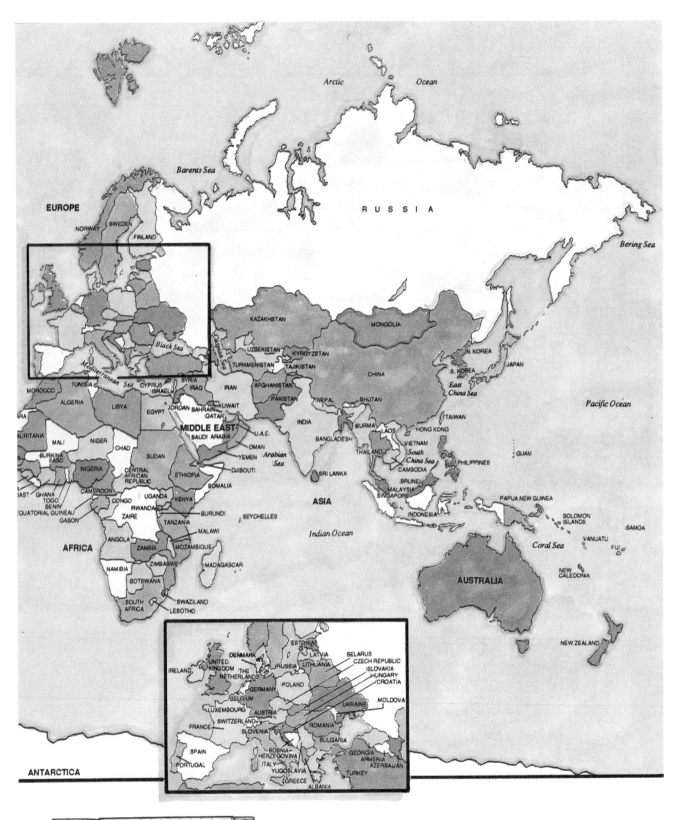

A. Where's ....?   A. What ocean/sea is near
B. It's in _____.   ....?

A. What do you do every day?
B. I **get up**, I **take a shower**, and I **brush my teeth**.

вставать	**1.** get up
принимать душ	**2.** take a shower
чистить зубы	**3.** brush *my** teeth
чистить между зубами	**4.** floss *my** teeth
бриться	**5.** shave
одеться	**6.** get dressed
мыть лицо	**7.** wash *my** face
положить косметику	**8.** put on makeup
причесать волосы	**9.** brush *my** hair
расчёсывать волосы	**10.** comb *my** hair
застелить постель	**11.** make the bed

раздеться	**12.** get undressed
принять ванну	**13.** take a bath
ложиться спать	**14.** go to bed
спать	**15.** sleep
готовить завтрак	**16.** make breakfast
готовить обед	**17.** make lunch
готовить ужин	**18.** cook/make dinner
завтракать	**19.** eat/have breakfast
обедать	**20.** eat/have lunch
ужинать	**21.** eat/have dinner

*my, his, her, our, your, their

A. What does he do every day?
B. He _____s, he _____s, and he _____s.

A. What does she do every day?
B. She _____s, she _____s, and she _____s.

What do you do every day? Make a list.
Interview some friends and tell about their everyday activities.

ВИДЫ ПОВСЕДНЕВНОЙ ДЕЯТЕЛЬНОСТИ II

A. Hi! What are you doing?
B. I'm **clean**ing **the apartment**.

убирать в квартире/доме	**1.**	clean the apartment/ clean the house
подметать пол	**2.**	sweep the floor
протереть пыль	**3.**	dust
пылесосить	**4.**	vacuum
мыть посуду	**5.**	wash the dishes
стирать	**6.**	do the laundry
гладить	**7.**	iron
кормить ребёнка	**8.**	feed the baby
кормить кошку	**9.**	feed the cat
выгуливать собаку	**10.**	walk the dog
смотреть телевизор	**11.**	watch TV
слушать радио	**12.**	listen to the radio
слушать музыку	**13.**	listen to music
читать	**14.**	read
играть	**15.**	play
играть в баскетбол	**16.**	play basketball
играть на гитаре	**17.**	play the guitar
упражняться на пианино	**18.**	practice the piano
заниматься	**19.**	study
делать упражнения	**20.**	exercise

A. Hi, ...! This is ....
   What are you doing?
B. I'm _____ing. How about you?
A. I'm _____ing.

A. Are you going to _____ today?
B. Yes. I'm going to _____ in a
   little while.

What are you going to do tomorrow?
Make a list of *everything* you are
going to do.

КЛАССНАЯ КОМНАТА

A. Where's the **teacher**?
B. The **teacher** is *next to* the **board**.

A. Where's the **pen**?
B. The **pen** is *on* the **desk**.

учитель	**1.** teacher	доска	**18.** board
помощник учителя	**2.** teacher's aide	мел	**19.** chalk
ученик/ученица/учащийся	**3.** student	полка для мела	**20.** chalk tray
стул	**4.** seat/chair	тряпка для доски	**21.** eraser
ручка	**5.** pen	громкоговоритель	**22.** P.A. system/loudspeaker
карандаш	**6.** pencil	доска для объявлений	**23.** bulletin board
ластик/стирательная резина	**7.** eraser	кнопка	**24.** thumbtack
парта	**8.** desk	карта	**25.** map
учительский стол	**9.** teacher's desk	точилка	**26.** pencil sharpener
учебник	**10.** book/textbook	глобус	**27.** globe
тетрадь	**11.** notebook	книжная полка	**28.** bookshelf
бумага в линейку	**12.** notebook paper	проектор	**29.** overhead projector
бумага в клетку	**13.** graph paper	телевизор	**30.** TV
линейка	**14.** ruler	киноэкран	**31.** (movie) screen
калькулятор	**15.** calculator	проектор для слайдов	**32.** slide projector
часы	**16.** clock	компьютер	**33.** computer
флаг	**17.** flag	кинопроектор	**34.** (movie) projector

A. Is there a/an _____ in your classroom?*
B. Yes. There's a/an _____ next to/on the _____.

A. Is there a/an _____ in your classroom?*
B. No, there isn't.

Describe your classroom.
(There's a/an ....)

*With 12, 13, 19 use: Is there _____ in your classroom?

КЛАССНЫЕ ВИДЫ ДЕЯТЕЛЬНОСТИ

Встань.	**1.** Stand up.
Иди к *доске*.	**2.** Go to the *board*.
Напиши *своё имя*.	**3.** Write *your name*.
Сотри *своё имя*.	**4.** Erase *your name*.
Садись.	**5.** Sit down./Take your seat.
Открой *свою книгу*.	**6.** Open *your book*.
Читай *восьмую страницу*.	**7.** Read *page eight*.
Изучай *восьмую страницу*.	**8.** Study *page eight*.
Закрой *свою книгу*.	**9.** Close *your book*.
Убери *свою книгу*.	**10.** Put away *your book*.
Слушай *вопрос*.	**11.** Listen to *the question*.
Подними *руку*.	**12.** Raise *your hand*.
Отвечай.	**13.** Give *the answer*.
Работайте *группами*.	**14.** Work *in groups*.
Помогите *друг другу*.	**15.** Help *each other*.

Делай *домашнюю работу*.	**16.** Do *your homework*.
Принеси *домашнюю работу*.	**17.** Bring in *your homework*.
Проверь *ответы*.	**18.** Go over *the answers*.
Исправь *свои ошибки*.	**19.** Correct *your mistakes*.
Сдай *домашнюю работу*.	**20.** Hand in *your homework*.
Достань *лист бумаги*.	**21.** Take out *a piece of paper*.
Раздай *тесты*.	**22.** Pass out *the tests*.
Отвечай на *вопросы*.	**23.** Answer *the questions*.
Проверь *свои ответы*.	**24.** Check *your answers*.
Собери *тесты*.	**25.** Collect *the tests*.
Опусти *шторы*.	**26.** Lower *the shades*.
Выключи *свет*.	**27.** Turn off *the lights*.
Включи *проектор*.	**28.** Turn on *the projector*.
Смотри *кино*.	**29.** Watch *the movie*.
Записывай.	**30.** Take notes.

You're the teacher! Give instructions to your students.

A. Where are you from?
B. I'm from **Mexico**.

A. What's your nationality?
B. I'm **Mexican**.

A. What language do you speak?
B. I speak **Spanish**.

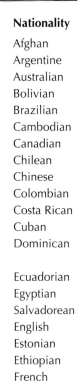

Country	Nationality	Language	Country	Nationality	Language
Afghanistan	Afghan	Afghan	Italy	Italian	Italian
Argentina	Argentine	Spanish	Japan	Japanese	Japanese
Australia	Australian	English	Jordan	Jordanian	Arabic
Bolivia	Bolivian	Spanish	Korea	Korean	Korean
Brazil	Brazilian	Portuguese	Laos	Laotian	Laotian
Cambodia	Cambodian	Cambodian	Latvia	Latvian	Latvian
Canada	Canadian	English/French	Lithuania	Lithuanian	Lithuanian
Chile	Chilean	Spanish	Malaysia	Malaysian	Malay
China	Chinese	Chinese	Mexico	Mexican	Spanish
Colombia	Colombian	Spanish	New Zealand	New Zealander	English
Costa Rica	Costa Rican	Spanish	Nicaragua	Nicaraguan	Spanish
Cuba	Cuban	Spanish	Panama	Panamanian	Spanish
(The) Dominican Republic	Dominican	Spanish	Peru	Peruvian	Spanish
Ecuador	Ecuadorian	Spanish	(The) Philippines	Filipino	Tagalog
Egypt	Egyptian	Arabic	Poland	Polish	Polish
El Salvador	Salvadorean	Spanish	Portugal	Portuguese	Portuguese
England	English	English	Puerto Rico	Puerto Rican	Spanish
Estonia	Estonian	Estonian	Romania	Romanian	Romanian
Ethiopia	Ethiopian	Amharic	Russia	Russian	Russian
France	French	French	Saudi Arabia	Saudi	Arabic
Germany	German	German	Spain	Spanish	Spanish
Greece	Greek	Greek	Taiwan	Taiwanese	Chinese
Guatemala	Guatemalan	Spanish	Thailand	Thai	Thai
Haiti	Haitian	Haitian Kreyol	Turkey	Turkish	Turkish
Honduras	Honduran	Spanish	Ukraine	Ukrainian	Ukrainian
Indonesia	Indonesian	Indonesian	(The) United States	American	English
Israel	Israeli	Hebrew	Venezuela	Venezuelan	Spanish
			Vietnam	Vietnamese	Vietnamese

A. What's your native language?
B. _____.
A. Oh. What country are you from?
B. _____.

A. Where are you and your husband/wife going on your vacation?
B. We're going to _____.
A. That's nice. Tell me, do you speak _____?
B. No, but my husband/wife does. He's/She's _____.

Tell about yourself:
   Where are you from?
   What's your nationality?
   What languages do you speak?
Now interview and tell about a friend.

ВИДЫ ЖИЛЬЯ

A. Where do you live?
B. I live in an **apartment building**.

квартира	**1.** apartment (building)	дом на колёсах	**7.** mobile home/trailer
дом	**2.** (single-family) house	фермерский дом	**8.** farmhouse
дом на две семьи	**3.** duplex/two-family house	хижина	**9.** cabin
городской дом	**4.** townhouse/townhome	дом (для) престарелых	**10.** nursing home
кондоминиум	**5.** condominimum/condo	приют	**11.** shelter
общежитие	**6.** dormitory/dorm	плавучий дом	**12.** houseboat

A. Town Taxi Company.
B. Hello. Please send a taxi to
   (address) .
A. Is that a house or an apartment?
B. It's a/an _____.
A. All right. We'll be there right
   away.

A. This is the Emergency Operator.
B. Please send an ambulance to
   (address) .
A. Is that a private home?
B. It's a/an _____.
A. What's your name?
B. ....
A. And your telephone number?
B. ....

Tell about people you know and the
types of housing they live in.
Discuss:
   Who lives in dormitories?
   Who lives in nursing homes?
   Who lives in shelters?
   Why?

ГОСТИНАЯ КОМНАТА

A. Where are you?
B. I'm in the living room.
A. What are you doing?
B. I'm *dusting** the **coffee table**.

*dusting/cleaning

кофейный стол	**1.** coffee table		телевизор	**15.** television
ковёр	**2.** rug		видеомагнитофон	**16.** video cassette recorder/VCR
пол	**3.** floor		стереосистема	**17.** stereo system
кресло	**4.** armchair		громкоговоритель	**18.** speaker
столик	**5.** end table		кресло для двоих	**19.** loveseat
лампа	**6.** lamp		растение	**20.** plant
абажур	**7.** lampshade		картина	**21.** painting
окно	**8.** window		рама	**22.** frame
шторы	**9.** drapes/curtains		каминная полка	**23.** mantel
диван	**10.** sofa/couch		камин	**24.** fireplace
подушка	**11.** (throw) pillow		каминный экран	**25.** fireplace screen
потолок	**12.** ceiling		фотография	**26.** picture/photograph
стена	**13.** wall		книжный шкаф	**27.** bookcase
стенка	**14.** wall unit/entertainment unit			

A. You have a lovely living room!
B. Oh, thank you.
A. Your _____ is/are beautiful!
B. Thank you for saying so.

A. Uh-oh! I just spilled coffee on your _____!
B. That's okay. Don't worry about it.

Tell about your living room.
(In my living room there's ....)

СТОЛОВАЯ КОМНАТА

A. This **dining room table** is very nice.
B. Thank you. It was a gift from my *grandmother.* *

*grandmother/grandfather/aunt/uncle/...

стол	**1.** (dining room) table	подсвечник	**12.** candlestick
стул	**2.** (dining room) chair	свеча	**13.** candle
сервант	**3.** china cabinet	ваза в центре стола	**14.** centerpiece
фарфор	**4.** china	солонка	**15.** salt shaker
люстра/канделябр	**5.** chandelier	перечница	**16.** pepper shaker
буфет/сервант	**6.** buffet	маслёнка	**17.** butter dish
чаша для салата	**7.** salad bowl	передвижной столик	**18.** serving cart
кувшин	**8.** pitcher	чайник	**19.** teapot
большая чаша	**9.** serving bowl	кофейник	**20.** coffee pot
поднос	**10.** serving platter	кувшинчик для сливок	**21.** creamer
скатерть	**11.** tablecloth	сахарница	**22.** sugar bowl

[In a store]

A. May I help you?
B. Yes, please. Do you have
   _____s? *
A. Yes. _____s* are right over there.
B. Thank you.

*With 4, use the singular.

[At home]

A. Look at this old _____
   I just bought!
B. Where did you buy it?
A. At a yard sale. How do you
   like it?
B. It's VERY unusual!

Tell about your dining room.
(In my dining room there's ....)

СТОЛОВАЯ: НАКРЫТИЕ СТОЛА

A. Excuse me. Where does the **salad plate** go?
B. It goes *to the left of* the **dinner plate**.

A. Excuse me. Where does the **soup spoon** go?
B. It goes *to the right of* the **teaspoon**.

A. Excuse me. Where does the **wine glass** go?
B. It goes *between* the **water glass** and the **cup and saucer**.

A. Excuse me. Where does the **cup** go?
B. It goes *on* the **saucer**.

тарелка для салата	**1.** salad plate	настольные приборы	**silverware**
тарелка для хлеба и масла	**2.** bread-and-butter plate	вилка для салата	**10.** salad fork
тарелка для ужина	**3.** dinner plate	вилка для ужина	**11.** dinner fork
супная тарелка	**4.** soup bowl	нож	**12.** knife
стакан для воды	**5.** water glass	чайная ложка	**13.** teaspoon
бокал/рюмка	**6.** wine glass	ложка для супа	**14.** soup spoon
чашка	**7.** cup	нож для масла	**15.** butter knife
блюдце	**8.** saucer		
салфетка	**9.** napkin		

A. Waiter? Excuse me. This _____ is dirty.
B. I'm terribly sorry. I'll get you another _____ right away.

A. Oops! I dropped my _____!
B. That's okay! I'll get you another _____ from the kitchen.

Practice giving directions. Tell someone how to set a table. (Put the ....)

A. Ooh! Look at that big bug!!
B. Where?
A. It's on the **bed**!
B. I'LL get it.

кровать/постель	**1.** bed	зеркало	**18.** mirror
спинка	**2.** headboard	шкатулка для драгоценностей	**19.** jewelry box
подушка	**3.** pillow	комод для белья	**20.** dresser/bureau
наволочка	**4.** pillowcase	односпальная кровать	**21.** twin bed
простыня	**5.** fitted sheet	матрац	**22.** mattress
простыня	**6.** (flat) sheet	пружинный матрац	**23.** box spring
одеяло	**7.** blanket	двухспальная кровать	**24.** double bed
электрическое одеяло	**8.** electric blanket	двухспальная кровать	**25.** queen-size bed
тряпочка для пыли	**9.** dust ruffle	двухспальная кровать	**26.** king-size bed
покрывало	**10.** bedspread	койка	**27.** bunk bed
стёганое одеяло	**11.** comforter/quilt	кровать с выдвижным ящиком	**28.** trundle bed
спинка	**12.** footboard	диван-кровать	**29.** sofa bed/convertible sofa
шторы	**13.** blinds	кушетка	**30.** day bed
ночной столик	**14.** night table/nightstand	раскладушка	**31.** cot
будильник	**15.** alarm clock	кровать с водяным матрацом	**32.** water bed
радиоприёмник с часами	**16.** clock radio	кровать с балдахином	**33.** canopy bed
комод	**17.** chest (of drawers)	больничная койка	**34.** hospital bed

[In a store]

A. Excuse me. I'm looking for a/an _____.*
B. We have some very nice _____s. And they're all on sale this week.
A. Oh, good!

*With 13, use: Excuse me. I'm looking for _____.

[In a bedroom]

A. Oh, no! I just lost my contact lens!
B. Where?
A. I think it's on the _____.
B. I'll help you look.

Tell about your bedroom.
(In my bedroom there's ....)

КУХНЯ

A. I think we need a new **dishwasher**.
B. I think you're right.

посудомойка	**1.** dishwasher	жестяная коробка	**18.** canister
моющее средство	**2.** dishwasher detergent	кухонная плита	**19.** stove/range
жидкое моющее средство	**3.** dishwashing liquid	горелка	**20.** burner
кран	**4.** faucet	печь/духовка	**21.** oven
раковина	**5.** (kitchen) sink	тряпка для горячей посуды	**22.** potholder
мусоропровод	**6.** (garbage) disposal	тостер	**23.** toaster
губка	**7.** sponge	полка для специй	**24.** spice rack
металлическая щётка	**8.** scouring pad	электрооткрывалка	**25.** (electric) can opener
щётка	**9.** pot scrubber	кулинарная книга	**26.** cookbook
подставка для посуды	**10.** dish rack	холодильник	**27.** refrigerator
держатель бумажных салфет	**11.** paper towel holder	морозилка	**28.** freezer
полотенце для посуды	**12.** dish towel	изготовитель льда	**29.** ice maker
ящик для мусора	**13.** trash compactor	поддон/резервуар для льда	**30.** ice tray
шкаф	**14.** cabinet	магнит для холодильника	**31.** refrigerator magnet
микроволновая печь	**15.** microwave (oven)	кухонный стол	**32.** kitchen table
покрытие над всеми столами	**16.** (kitchen) counter	салфетка	**33.** placemat
кухонная доска	**17.** cutting board	кухонный стул	**34.** kitchen chair
		мусорное ведро	**35.** garbage pail

[In a store]

A. Excuse me. Are your _____s still on sale?
B. Yes, they are. They're twenty percent off.

[In a kitchen]

A. When did you get this/these new _____(s)?
B. I got it/them last week.

Tell about your kitchen.
(In my kitchen there's ....)

КУХОННЫЕ ПРИБОРЫ

A. Could I possibly borrow your **wok**?
B. Sure. I'll get it for you right now.
A. Thanks.

вок	**1.** wok
кастрюля	**2.** pot
кастрюля с ручкой	**3.** saucepan
крышка	**4.** lid/cover/top
сковорода	**5.** frying pan/skillet
жаровня без крышки	**6.** roasting pan
жаровня	**7.** roaster
двойная кастрюля	**8.** double boiler
скороварка	**9.** pressure cooker
дуршлаг	**10.** colander
кастрюлечка	**11.** casserole (dish)
форма для печки тортов	**12.** cake pan
форма для пирогов	**13.** pie plate
поднос для печенья	**14.** cookie sheet
чаша для смешивания	**15.** (mixing) bowl
скалка	**16.** rolling pin
измерительная чашка	**17.** measuring cup
измерительная ложка	**18.** measuring spoon
кофейная машина	**19.** coffeemaker
кофемолка	**20.** coffee grinder
чайник	**21.** tea kettle
тостер-печка	**22.** toaster oven

электромиксер	**23.** (electric) mixer
кухонный комбайн	**24.** food processor
электросковорода	**25.** electric frying pan
вафельница	**26.** waffle iron
электросковорода	**27.** (electric) griddle
изготовитель воздушной кукурузы	**28.** popcorn maker
смеситель	**29.** blender
тёрка	**30.** grater
сбивалка	**31.** (egg) beater
ковш/черпак	**32.** ladle
ковшик для мороженого	**33.** ice cream scoop
формочка	**34.** cookie cutter
сито	**35.** strainer
давилка для чеснока	**36.** garlic press
открывалка	**37.** bottle opener
консервный нож	**38.** can opener
мутовка	**39.** whisk
нож для овощей	**40.** (vegetable) peeler
нож	**41.** knife
лопаточка/шпатель	**42.** spatula
маленький нож	**43.** paring knife

A. What are you looking for?
B. I'm looking for the _____.*
A. Did you look in the drawers/ in the cabinets/next to the _____/..........?
B. Yes. I looked everywhere!

*With 2, 4, 12–15, 41, use:
  I'm looking for a _____.

[A Commercial]
Come to *Kitchen World*! We have everything you need for your kitchen, from _____s and _____s, to _____s and _____s. Are you looking for a new _____? Is it time to throw out your old _____? Come to *Kitchen World* today! We have everything you need!

What things do you have in your kitchen?
Which things do you use very often?
Which things do you rarely use?

A. Thank you for the **teddy bear.** It's a very nice gift.
B. You're welcome. Tell me, when are you due?
A. In a few more weeks.

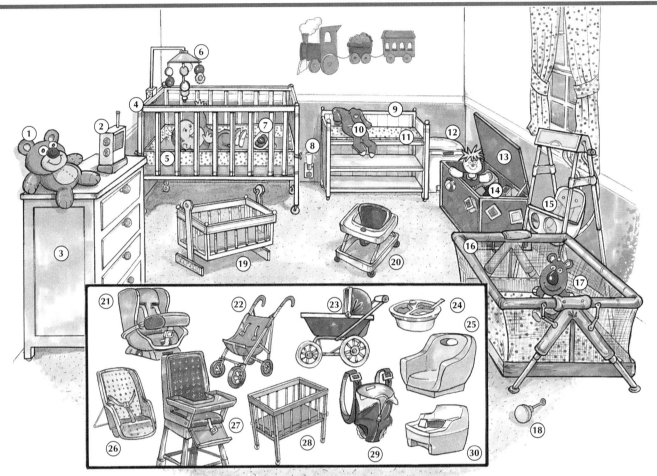

мишка	**1.** teddy bear	детский манеж	**16.** playpen
переговорное устройство	**2.** intercom	игрушка	**17.** stuffed animal
комод	**3.** chest (of drawers)	погремушка	**18.** rattle
детская кровать	**4.** crib	колыбель/люлька	**19.** cradle
перегородка	**5.** crib bumper	ходунки	**20.** walker
подвесная игрушка	**6.** mobile	автосиденье	**21.** car seat
кроватная игрушка	**7.** crib toy	прогулочная коляска	**22.** stroller
ночная лампа	**8.** night light	детская коляска	**23.** baby carriage
столик для пеленания	**9.** changing table/ dressing table	устройство для подогрева пищи	**24.** food warmer
		возвышенный стул	**25.** booster seat
детский костюм	**10.** stretch suit	детский стул	**26.** baby seat
подстилка для переодевания	**11.** changing pad	высокий стул	**27.** high chair
корзина для пелёнок	**12.** diaper pail	передвижная кроватка	**28.** portable crib
ящик для игрушек	**13.** toy chest	рюкзак для переноски детей	**29.** baby carrier
кукла	**14.** doll	горшок	**30.** potty
качели	**15.** swing		

A. That's a very nice _____.
   Where did you get it?
B. It was a gift from ....

A. Do you have everything you
   need before the baby comes?
B. Almost everything. We're still
   looking for a/an _____ and
   a/an _____.

Tell about your country:
   What things do people buy for a
   new baby?
   Does a new baby sleep in a separate
   room, as in the United States?

УХОД ЗА ДЕТЬМИ

[1–12]
A. Do we need anything from the store?
B. Yes. Could you get some more **baby powder**?
A. Sure.

[13–17]
A. Do we need anything from the store?
B. Yes. Could you get another **pacifier**?
A. Sure.

детская пудра	**1.** baby powder	одноразовые пелёнки	**10.** disposable diapers
детский лосьон	**2.** baby lotion	пелёнки из материи	**11.** cloth diapers
детский шампунь	**3.** baby shampoo	жидкие витамины	**12.** (liquid) vitamins
мазь	**4.** ointment	соска/пустышка	**13.** pacifier
детская формула	**5.** formula	рожок	**14.** bottle
детское питание	**6.** baby food	соска	**15.** nipple
мягкие салфетки	**7.** (baby) wipes	нагрудник	**16.** bib
полоски с ватными концами	**8.** cotton swabs	зубное кольцо	**17.** teething ring
булавки для пелёнок	**9.** diaper pins		

[In a store]
A. Excuse me. I can't find the _____.*
B. I'm sorry. We're out of _____.* We'll have some more tomorrow.

[At home]
A. Honey? Where did you put the _____?
B. It's/They're in/on/next to the _____.

In your opinion, which are better: cloth diapers or disposable diapers? Why?
Tell about baby products in your country.

*With 13–17, use the plural.

A. Where's the **plunger**?
B. It's *next to* the **toilet**.

A. Where's the **toothbrush**?
B. It's *in* the **toothbrush holder**.

A. Where's the **washcloth**?
B. It's *on* the **towel rack**.

A. Where's the **mirror**?
B. It's *over* the **sink**.

плунжер	**1.** plunger	фен	**16.** hair dryer	набор для чистки зубов	**29.** Water Pik
унитаз	**2.** toilet	вентилятор	**17.** fan	шкафчик под раковиной	**30.** vanity
туалетный бак	**3.** toilet tank	зеркало	**18.** mirror	корзина для мусора	**31.** wastebasket
туалетное сиденье	**4.** toilet seat	аптечка	**19.** medicine cabinet/ medicine chest	душ	**32.** shower
освежитель воздуха	**5.** air freshener	раковина	**20.** (bathroom) sink	палка для занавеса	**33.** shower curtain rod
держатель туалетной бумаги	**6.** toilet paper holder	кран для горячей воды	**21.** hot water faucet	душевой кран	**34.** shower head
туалетная бумага	**7.** toilet paper	кран для холодной воды	**22.** cold water faucet	кольца	**35.** shower curtain rings
туалетная щётка	**8.** toilet brush	стакан	**23.** cup	душевой занавес	**36.** shower curtain
вешалка для полотенец	**9.** towel rack	зубная щётка	**24.** toothbrush	ванная	**37.** bathtub/tub
ванное полотенце	**10.** bath towel	держатель для зубных щёток	**25.** toothbrush holder	сток/водосток	**38.** drain
полотенце для рук	**11.** hand towel	мыло	**26.** soap	резиновый коврик	**39.** rubber mat
маленькое полотенце	**12.** washcloth/face cloth	мыльница	**27.** soap dish	губка	**40.** sponge
корзина для белья	**13.** hamper	резервуар с мылом	**28.** soap dispenser	ванный коврик	**41.** bath mat/bath rug
весы	**14.** (bathroom) scale				
полка	**15.** shelf				

A. [Knock. Knock.] Did I leave my glasses in there?
B. Yes. They're on/in/next to the _____.

A. *Bobby?*
B. Yes, Mom/Dad?
A. You didn't clean up the bathroom! There's toothpaste on the _____ and there's powder all over the _____!
B. Sorry, Mom/Dad. I'll clean it up right away.

Tell about your bathroom.
(In my bathroom there's ....)

ПРОДУКТЫ ДЛЯ ПЕРСОНАЛЬНОГО УХОДА

[1–17]
A. Excuse me. Where can I find **toothbrush**es?
B. They're in the next aisle.
A. Thank you.

[18–38]
A. Excuse me. Where can I find **shampoo**?
B. It's in the next aisle.
A. Thank you.

зубная щётка	**1.** toothbrush	заколки для волос	**15.** bobby pins	пудра	**27.** powder
расчёска/гребень	**2.** comb	клипсы для волос	**16.** hair clips	лосьон для рук	**28.** hand lotion
щётка	**3.** (hair) brush	декоративные	**17.** barrettes	духи/одеколон	**29.** perfume/cologne
бритва	**4.** razor	заколки		крем для обуви	**30.** shoe polish
лезвия	**5.** razor blades	шампунь	**18.** shampoo	лак для ногтей	**31.** nail polish
электробритва	**6.** electric razor/ electric shaver	кондиционер	**19.** conditioner/rinse	раствор для снятия лака	**32.** nail polish remover
кровоостанавливающий карандаш	**7.** styptic pencil	держатель для волос	**20.** hairspray		
душевая шапочка	**8.** shower cap	зубная паста	**21.** toothpaste	косметика	**makeup**
пилка	**9.** nail file	жидкость для полоскания рта	**22.** mouthwash	крем под пудру	**33.** base/foundation
пилка для ногтей	**10.** emery board	нить для чистки зубов	**23.** dental floss	румяна	**34.** blush/rouge
щипцы для ногтей	**11.** nail clipper			губная помада	**35.** lipstick
щётка для ногтей	**12.** nail brush	крем для бритья	**24.** shaving creme	тени	**36.** eye shadow
ножницы	**13.** scissors	лосьон после бритья	**25.** after shave lotion	косметический карандаш	**37.** eye liner
пинцет/щипчики	**14.** tweezers	дезодоратор	**26.** deodorant	тушь для ресниц	**38.** mascara

---

A. I'm going to the drug store to get a/an _____.*
B. While you're there, could you also get a/an _____?*
A. Sure.

*With 5, 13–38, use: get _____.

A. Do you have everything for the trip?
B. I think so.
A. Did you remember to pack your _____?
B. Oops! I forgot. Thanks for reminding me.

You're going on a trip. Make a list of personal care products you need to take with you.

ЧИСТКА ПО ДОМУ И СТИРКА ОДЕЖДЫ

[1–17, 28–39]
A. Excuse me. Do you sell **broom**s?
B. Yes. They're at the back of the store.
A. Thanks.

[18–27]
A. Excuse me. Do you sell **laundry detergent**?
B. Yes. It's at the back of the store.
A. Thanks.

метла	**1.** broom	швабра для пыли	**13.** (dust) mop/ (dry) mop	аммиачный раствор	**25.** ammonia
совок	**2.** dustpan			лак для мебели	**26.** furniture polish
метёлочка	**3.** whisk broom	швабра для пола	**14.** (sponge) mop	воск для пола	**27.** floor wax
щётка для пыли	**4.** feather duster	швабра	**15.** (wet) mop	бумажные салфетки	**28.** paper towels
тряпка для пыли	**5.** dust cloth	стиральная	**16.** washing machine/ washer	вешалка	**29.** hanger
утюг	**6.** iron	машина		бельевая корзина	**30.** laundry basket
гладильная	**7.** ironing board	сушилка	**17.** dryer	мешок для белья	**31.** laundry bag
доска		стиральный	**18.** laundry detergent	раковина	**32.** utility sink
механический	**8.** carpet sweeper	порошок		щётка	**33.** scrub brush
пылесос		смягчитель	**19.** fabric softener	губка	**34.** sponge
пылесос	**9.** vacuum (cleaner)	отбеливатель	**20.** bleach	ведро	**35.** bucket/pail
части для	**10.** vacuum cleaner attachments	крахмал	**21.** starch	ящик для мусора	**36.** trash can/ garbage can
пылесоса		салфетка для	**22.** static cling remover		
пакет для	**11.** vacuum cleaner bag	снятия статики		ящик для вторсырья	**37.** recycling bin
мусора		моющее средство	**23.** cleanser	бельевая верёвка	**38.** clothesline
ручной пылесос	**12.** hand vacuum	оконное моющее	**24.** window cleaner	бельевая прищепка	**39.** clothespins
		средство			

A. How do you like this/these
_____?
B. It's/They're great!

A. They're having a big sale at Dave's Discount Store this week.
B. Oh, really? What's on sale?
A. _[18–27]_ and _[1–17, 28–39]_ s.

Who does the cleaning and laundry in your home? What things does that person use?

ВНЕ ДОМА

A. When are you going to repair the **lamppost**?
B. I'm going to repair it next Saturday.

фонарный столб	**1.** lamppost		гаражная дверь	**17.** garage door
почтовый ящик	**2.** mailbox		дорога к гаражу	**18.** driveway
передняя дорожка	**3.** front walk		водосточный жёлоб	**19.** gutter
передние ступеньки	**4.** front steps		дренажная труба	**20.** drainpipe/downspout
передняя веранда	**5.** (front) porch		веранда	**21.** deck
наружная дверь	**6.** storm door		задняя дверь	**22.** back door
входная дверь	**7.** front door		дверная ручка	**23.** doorknob
дверной звонок	**8.** doorbell		дверь с сеткой	**24.** screen door
лампа	**9.** (front) light		боковая дверь	**25.** side door
окно	**10.** window		параболическая антенна	**26.** satellite dish
сетка	**11.** (window) screen		патио/дворик	**27.** patio
ставень	**12.** shutter		газонокосилка	**28.** lawnmower
крыша	**13.** roof		ражпер	**29.** barbecue/(outdoor) grill
телевизионная антенна	**14.** TV antenna		стул для газона	**30.** lawn chair
труба/дымоход	**15.** chimney		сарай для инструмента	**31.** tool shed
гараж	**16.** garage			

[On the telephone]
A. Harry's Home Repairs.
B. Hello. Do you fix _____s?
A. No, we don't.
B. Oh, okay. Thank you.

[At work on Monday morning]
A. What did you do this weekend?
B. Nothing much. I repaired my _____ and my _____.

Do you like to repair things?
What things can you repair yourself?
What things can't you repair? Who repairs them?

МНОГОКВАРТИРНЫЙ ДОМ

A. Is there a **lobby**?
B. Yes, there is. Do you want to see the apartment?
A. Yes, I do.

вестибюль	**1.** lobby		ножарная тревога	**12.** fire alarm
внутренняя связь	**2.** intercom		мусоропровод	**13.** garbage chute
звонок	**3.** buzzer		комната для стирки	**14.** laundry room
почтовый ящик	**4.** mailbox		домоуправ	**15.** superintendent
лифт	**5.** elevator		комната для хранения	**16.** storage room
швейцар	**6.** doorman		стоянка-гараж	**17.** parking garage
дымодетектор	**7.** smoke detector		автостоянка	**18.** parking lot
глазок	**8.** peephole		балкон/терраса	**19.** balcony/terrace
дверная цепочка	**9.** (door) chain		бассейн	**20.** swimming pool
замок	**10.** dead-bolt lock		ванна с бурлящей водой	**21.** whirlpool
кондиционер воздуха	**11.** air conditioner			

[Renting an apartment]

A. Let me show you around the building.*
B. Okay.
A. This is the _____ and here's the _____.
B. I see.

*With 7–11, use:
  Let me show you around the apartment.

[On the telephone]

A. Mom and Dad? I found an apartment.
B. Good. Tell us about it.
A. It has a/an _____ and a/an _____.
B. That's nice. Does it have a/an _____?
A. Yes, it does.

Tell about the differences between living in a house and in an apartment building.

A. Did you remember to pay the **carpenter**?
B. Yes. I wrote a check yesterday.

плотник	1. carpenter	счёт за газ	12. gas bill
разнорабочий	2. handyman	счёт за электричество	13. electric bill
маляр	3. (house) painter	счёт за телефон	14. telephone bill
трубочист	4. chimney sweep	счёт за воду	15. water bill
мастер по ремонту бытовых приборов	5. appliance repair person	счёт за тепло	16. oil bill/heating bill
телевизионщик	6. TV repair person	счёт за кабельное телевидение	17. cable TV bill
слесарь	7. locksmith	счёт за дезинфекцию	18. pest control bill
садовник	8. gardener	арендная плата	19. rent
электрик	9. electrician	плата за парковку	20. parking fee
водопроводчик	10. plumber	плата по закладной	21. mortgage payment
дезинсектор	11. exterminator		

[1–11]

A. When is the _____ going to come?
B. This afternoon.

[12–21]

A. When is the _____ due?
B. It's due at the end of the month.

Tell about utilities, services, and repairs you pay for. How much do you pay?

ИНСТРУМЕНТЫ

A. Could I borrow your **hammer***?
B. Sure.
A. Thanks.

With 28–32, use: Could I borrow some _____ s?

молоток	**1.** hammer	стаместка/зубило	**12.** chisel	кисть	**23.** paintbrush/brush
отвёртка	**2.** screwdriver	скребок	**13.** scraper	краска	**24.** paint
отвёртка	**3.** Phillips screwdriver	тиски	**14.** vise	разбавитель	**25.** paint thinner
Филлипс		электрическая	**15.** electric drill	наждачная бумага	**26.** sandpaper
гаечный ключ	**4.** wrench	дрель		проволока	**27.** wire
плоскогубцы	**5.** pliers	сверло/бур	**16.** (drill) bit	гвоздь	**28.** nail
ножовка	**6.** hacksaw	электропила	**17.** power saw	винт/шуруп	**29.** screw
топор	**7.** hatchet	нивелир/ватерпас	**18.** level	шайба	**30.** washer
разводной	**8.** monkey wrench	рубанок	**19.** plane	болт	**31.** bolt
гаечный ключ		ящик для	**20.** toolbox	гайка	**32.** nut
пила	**9.** saw	инструмента			
ручная дрель	**10.** hand drill	лоток	**21.** (paint) pan		
скрепа	**11.** brace	ролик	**22.** (paint) roller		

[1–4, 6–27]
A. Where's the _____?
B. It's on/next to/near/over/under the _____.

[5, 28–32]
A. Where are the _____(s)?
B. They're on/next to/near/over/under the _____.

Do you like to work with tools?
What tools do you have in your home?

[1–16]
A. I can't find the **lawnmower**!
B. Look in the tool shed.
A. I did.
B. Oh! Wait a minute! I lent the **lawnmower** to the neighbors.

[17–32]
A. I can't find the **flashlight**!
B. Look in the utility cabinet.
A. I did.
B. Oh! Wait a minute! I lent the **flashlight** to the neighbors.

газонокосилка	**1.** lawnmower	рабочие перчатки	**13.** work gloves	мышеловка	**24.** mousetrap
канистра	**2.** gas can	семена овощей	**14.** vegetable seeds	батарейки	**25.** batteries
разбрызгиватель	**3.** sprinkler	удобрение	**15.** fertilizer	лампочки	**26.** lightbulbs/bulbs
шланг	**4.** (garden) hose	семена травы	**16.** grass seed	пробки	**27.** fuses
носик шланга	**5.** nozzle	фонарь	**17.** flashlight	изолента	**28.** electrical tape
тачка	**6.** wheelbarrow	мухобойка	**18.** fly swatter	масло	**29.** oil
лейка	**7.** watering can	удлинитель	**19.** extension cord	клей	**30.** glue
грабли	**8.** rake	сантиметр/рулетка	**20.** tape measure	баллон с	**31.** bug spray/
мотыга	**9.** hoe	стремянка	**21.** step ladder	ядохимикатом	insect spray
совок	**10.** trowel	плунжер	**22.** plunger	ядохимикат от	**32.** roach killer
лопата	**11.** shovel	измерительная	**23.** yardstick	тараканов	
ножницы для	**12.** hedge clippers	линейка			
живой изгороди					

[1–11, 17–24]
A. I'm going to the hardware store. Can you think of anything we need?
B. Yes. We need a/an _____.
A. Oh, that's right.

[12–16, 25–32]
A. I'm going to the hardware store. Can you think of anything we need?
B. Yes. We need _____.
A. Oh, that's right.

What gardening tools and home supplies do you have? Tell about how and when you use each one.

ЧИСЛА

Количественные числа / **Cardinal Numbers**

1	one	11	eleven	21	twenty-one	101 one hundred (and) one
2	two	12	twelve	22	twenty-two	102 one hundred (and) two
3	three	13	thirteen	30	thirty	1,000 one thousand
4	four	14	fourteen	40	forty	10,000 ten thousand
5	five	15	fifteen	50	fifty	100,000 one hundred thousand
6	six	16	sixteen	60	sixty	1,000,000 one million
7	seven	17	seventeen	70	seventy	
8	eight	18	eighteen	80	eighty	
9	nine	19	nineteen	90	ninety	
10	ten	20	twenty	100	one hundred	

A. How old are you?
B. I'm _____ years old.

A. How many people are there in your family?
B. _____.

Порядковые числа / **Ordinal Numbers**

1st	first	11th	eleventh	21st	twenty-first	101st one hundred (and) first
2nd	second	12th	twelfth	22nd	twenty-second	102nd one hundred (and) second
3rd	third	13th	thirteenth	30th	thirtieth	1000th one thousandth
4th	fourth	14th	fourteenth	40th	fortieth	10,000th ten thousandth
5th	fifth	15th	fifteenth	50th	fiftieth	100,000th one hundred thousandth
6th	sixth	16th	sixteenth	60th	sixtieth	1,000,000th one millionth
7th	seventh	17th	seventeenth	70th	seventieth	
8th	eighth	18th	eighteenth	80th	eightieth	
9th	ninth	19th	nineteenth	90th	ninetieth	
10th	tenth	20th	twentieth	100th	one hundredth	

A. What floor do you live on?
B. I live on the _____ floor.

A. Is this the first time you've seen this movie?
B. No. It's the _____ time.

МАТЕМАТИКА

Арифметика / Arithmetic

suma addition   resta subtraction   multiplicación multiplication   división division

2 **plus** 1 **equals*** 3.   8 **minus** 3 **equals*** 5.   4 **times** 2 **equals*** 8.   10 **divided by** 2 **equals*** 5.

You can also say: **is**

A. How much is *two plus one*?
B. *Two plus one* equals/is *three*.

Make conversations for the arithmetic problems above and others.

Дробие / Fractions

one quarter/   one third   one half/   two thirds   three quarters/
one fourth   half   three fourths

A. Is this on sale?
B. Yes. It's _____ off the regular price.

A. Is the gas tank almost empty?
B. It's about _____ full.

Проценты / Percents

twenty-five percent   fifty percent   seventy-five percent   one hundred percent

A. How did you do on the test?
B. I got _____ percent of the answers right.

A. What's the weather forecast?
B. There's a _____ percent chance of rain.

Research and discuss:
What percentage of the people in your country live in cities?
live on farms? work in factories? vote in national elections?

ВРЕМЯ

 2:00

two o'clock

 2:15

two fifteen/
a quarter after *two*

 2:30

two thirty/
half past *two*

 2:45

two forty-five
a quarter to *three*

 2:05

two oh five

 2:20

two twenty/
twenty after *two*

 2:40

two forty/
twenty to *three*

 2:55

two fifty-five
five to *three*

A. What time is it?
B. It's _____.

A. What time does the movie begin?
B. At _____.

two a.m.

two p.m.

noon/
twelve noon

midnight/
twelve midnight

A. When does the train leave?
B. At _____.

A. What time will we arrive?
B. At _____.

Tell about your daily schedule:
    What do you do? When?
    (I get up at _____. I ....)
Do you usually have enough time to do things, or do you run
    out of time? Explain.
If there were 25 hours in a day, what would you do with the
    extra hour? Why?

Tell about the use of time in different cultures or countries
you are familiar with:
    Do people arrive on time for work? appointments? parties?
    Do trains and buses operate exactly on schedule?
    Do movies and sports events begin on time?
    Do workplaces use time clocks or timesheets to record
    employees' work hours?

JANUARY 1999

SUN	MON	TUE	WED	THUR	FRI	SAT
					1	2
3	4	5	6	7	8	9
10	11	12	13	14	15	16
17	18	19	20	21	22	23
24/31	25	26	27	28	29	30

1. year

год

тысяча девятьсот девяносто девятый год — nineteen ninety-nine

2. month

месяц

январь	January
февраль	February
март	March
апрель	April
май	May
июнь	June
июль	July
август	August
сентябрь	September
октябрь	October
ноябрь	November
декабрь	December

3. day

день недели

воскресенье	Sunday
понедельник	Monday
вторник	Tuesday
среда	Wednesday
четверг	Thursday
пятница	Friday
суббота	Saturday

4. date

дата/число

2 января 1999	January 2, 1999
2/1/99	1/2/99
второе января тысяча девятьсот девяносто девятого года	January second, nineteen ninety-nine

A. What year is it?
B. It's _____.

A. What month is it?
B. It's _____.

A. What day is it?
B. It's _____.

A. What's today's date?
B. Today is _____.

When did you begin to study English?
What days of the week do you study English? (I study English on _____.)

When is your birthday? (My birthday is on _____.)
What are your favorite months of the year? Why?
What are your least favorite months of the year? Why?

A. Where are you going?
B. I'm going to the **appliance store**.

магазин "Электроприборы"	**1.** appliance store		центр по уходу за детьми	**9.** child-care center/day-care center
торговец автомобилями	**2.** auto dealer/car dealer		химчистка	**10.** cleaners/dry cleaners
пекарня	**3.** bakery		пончиковый магазин	**11.** donut shop
банк	**4.** bank		поликлиника	**12.** clinic
парикмахерская	**5.** barber shop		магазин "Одежда"	**13.** clothing store
книжный магазин	**6.** book store		магазин "Кофе"	**14.** coffee shop
автобусная остановка	**7.** bus station		компьютерный магазин	**15.** computer store
кафетерий	**8.** cafeteria			

концертный зал	**16.** concert hall	мебельный магазин	**24.** furniture store
маленький магазин	**17.** convenience store	бензоколонка	**25.** gas station/ service station
копицентр	**18.** copy center		
гастроном	**19.** delicatessen/deli	продуктовый магазин	**26.** grocery store
универсам	**20.** department store	салон-парикмахерская	**27.** hair salon
магазин "Всё со скидкой"	**21.** discount store	хозяйственный магазин	**28.** hardware store
аптека	**22.** drug store/pharmacy	оздоровительный клуб	**29.** health club/spa
цветочный магазин	**23.** flower shop/florist	больница/госпиталь	**30.** hospital

A. Hi! How are you today?
B. Fine. Where are you going?
A. To the _____. How about you?
B. I'm going to the _____.

A. Oh, no! I can't find my wallet/purse!
B. Did you leave it at the _____?
A. Maybe I did.

Which of these places are in your neighborhood?
(In my neighborhood there's a/an ....)

ДОСТОПРИМЕЧАТЕЛЬНОСТИ ГОРОДА II

A. Where's the **hotel**?
B. It's right over there.

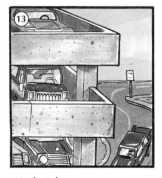

гостиница	**1.** hotel	музей	**9.** museum
кафе-мороженое	**2.** ice cream shop	музыкальный магазин	**10.** music store
ювелирный магазин	**3.** jewelry store	ночной клуб	**11.** night club
прачечная	**4.** laundromat	парк	**12.** park
библиотека	**5.** library	стоянка-гараж	**13.** (parking) garage
магазин для беременных женщин	**6.** maternity shop	автостоянка	**14.** parking lot
мотель	**7.** motel	зоомагазин	**15.** pet shop
кинотеатр	**8.** movie theater		

фотомагазин	**16.** photo shop		театр	**24.** theater
пиццерия	**17.** pizza shop		магазин игрушек	**25.** toy store
почта	**18.** post office		вокзал	**26.** train station
ресторан	**19.** restaurant		агентство путешествий	**27.** travel agency
школа	**20.** school		видеомагазин	**28.** video store
обувной магазин	**21.** shoe store		оптика	**29.** vision center/eyeglass store
торговый центр	**22.** (shopping) mall		зоопарк	**30.** zoo
супермаркет/универсам	**23.** supermarket			

A. Is there a/an _____ nearby?
B. Yes. There's a/an _____ around the corner.

A. Excuse me. Where's the _____?
B. It's down the street, next to the _____.
A. Thank you.

Which of these places are in your neighborhood?
(In my neighborhood there's a/an ....)

A. Where's the _____?
B. On/In/Next to/Between/Across from/ In front of/Behind/Under/Over the _____.

корзина для мусора	**1.** trash container		люк	**11.** manhole
отделение милиции	**2.** police station		автобусная остановка	**12.** bus stop
тюрьма	**3.** jail		такси	**13.** taxi/cab/taxicab
здание суда	**4.** courthouse		таксист	**14.** taxi driver/cab driver
скамья	**5.** bench		автобус	**15.** bus
уличный фонарь	**6.** street light		водитель автобуса	**16.** bus driver
грузовик-мороженое	**7.** ice cream truck		стояночный счётчик	**17.** parking meter
тротуар	**8.** sidewalk		женщина, проверяющая счётчики	**18.** meter maid
обочина	**9.** curb		метро	**19.** subway
улица	**10.** street		станция метро	**20.** subway station

электрический столб	**21.** utility pole		пожарный автосигнал	**30.** fire alarm box
стоянка такси	**22.** taxi stand		перекрёсток	**31.** intersection
телефонная будка	**23.** phone booth		милиционер	**32.** police officer
общественный телефон	**24.** public telephone		переход	**33.** crosswalk
сточная труба	**25.** sewer		пешеход	**34.** pedestrian
указательный знак	**26.** street sign		светофор	**35.** traffic light/traffic signal
пожарная станция	**27.** fire station		грузовик для мусора	**36.** garbage truck
ведомственное здание	**28.** office building		газетный киоск	**37.** newsstand
окно в проезде	**29.** drive-through window		уличный продавец	**38.** street vendor

[An Election Speech]

If I am elected mayor, I'll take care of all the problems we have in our city. We need to do something about our _____s. We also need to do something about our _____s. And look at our _____s! We REALLY need to do something about THEM! We need a new mayor who can solve these problems. If I am elected mayor, we'll be proud of our _____s, _____s, and _____s again! Vote for me!

Step outside. Look around.
Describe everything you see.

высокий – короткий/	**1–2**	tall – short
низкого роста		
длинный – короткий	**3–4**	long – short
большой – маленький	**5–6**	large/big – small/little
высокий – низкий	**7–8**	high – low
полный – худой	**9–10**	heavy/fat – thin/skinny
тяжёлый – лёгкий	**11–12**	heavy – light
свободный – узкий/тесный	**13–14**	loose – tight
быстрый – медленный	**15–16**	fast – slow
прямой – изогнутый	**17–18**	straight – crooked
прямой – кудрявый	**19–20**	straight – curly
широкий – узкий	**21–22**	wide – narrow
жирный – тонкий	**23–24**	thick – thin
тёмный – светлый	**25–26**	dark – light

новый – старый	**27–28**	new – old
молодой – старый	**29–30**	young – old
хороший – плохой	**31–32**	good – bad
горячий – холодный	**33–34**	hot – cold
мягкий – твёрдый	**35–36**	soft – hard
лёгкий – трудный	**37–38**	easy – difficult/hard
гладкий – шершавый	**39–40**	smooth – rough
аккуратный – неубранный	**41–42**	neat – messy
чистый – грязный	**43–44**	clean – dirty
шумный/громкий – тихий	**45–46**	noisy/loud – quiet
женатый/замужняя – холостой	**47–48**	married – single
богатый – бедный	**49–50**	rich/wealthy – poor

   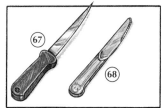

красивый – уродливый	**51–52** pretty/beautiful – ugly	дорогой – дешёвый	**61–62** expensive – cheap/inexpensive
красивый – уродливый	**53–54** handsome – ugly	нарядный – простой	**63–64** fancy – plain
мокрый – сухой	**55–56** wet – dry	блестящий – тусклый	**65–66** shiny – dull
открытый – закрытый	**57–58** open – closed	острый – тупой	**67–68** sharp – dull
полный – пустой	**59–60** full – empty		

[1–2]
A. Is your sister **tall**?
B. No. She's **short**.

1–2	Is your sister _____?
3–4	Is his hair _____?
5–6	Is their dog _____?
7–8	Is the bridge _____?
9–10	Is your friend _____?
11–12	Is the box _____?
13–14	Are the pants _____?
15–16	Is the train _____?
17–18	Is the path _____?
19–20	Is his hair _____?
21–22	Is that street _____?
23–24	Is the line _____?
25–26	Is the room _____?
27–28	Is your car _____?
29–30	Is he _____?
31–32	Are your neighbor's children _____?
33–34	Is the water _____?

35–36	Is your pillow _____?
37–38	Is today's homework _____?
39–40	Is your skin _____?
41–42	Is your desk _____?
43–44	Are the dishes _____?
45–46	Is your neighbor _____?
47–48	Is your sister _____?
49–50	Is your uncle _____?
51–52	Is the witch _____?
53–54	Is the pirate _____?
55–56	Are the clothes _____?
57–58	Is the door _____?
59–60	Is the pitcher _____?
61–62	Is that restaurant _____?
63–64	Is the dress _____?
65–66	Is your kitchen floor _____?
67–68	Is the knife _____?

A. Tell me about your ....
B. He's/She's/It's/They're _____.

A. Is your .... _____?
B. No, not at all. As a matter of fact, he's/she's/it's/they're _____.

Describe yourself.
Describe a person you know.
Describe one of your favorite places.

ОПИСАНИЕ ФИЗИЧЕСКИХ СОСТОЯНИЙ И ЭМОЦИЙ

A. You look **tired**.
B. I am. I'm VERY **tired**.

уставший	**1.** tired		больной	**9.** sick/ill
сонливый	**2.** sleepy		счастливый	**10.** happy
изнурённый	**3.** exhausted		радостный	**11.** ecstatic
(ему) жарко	**4.** hot		грустный	**12.** sad/unhappy
(ей) холодно	**5.** cold		несчастный	**13.** unlucky/unfortunate
голодный	**6.** hungry		довольный	**14.** pleased
испытывающий жажду	**7.** thirsty		разочарованный	**15.** disappointed
он наелся	**8.** full		огорчённый	**16.** upset

раздражённый	**17.** annoyed		озабоченный	**25.** worried
расстроенный	**18.** frustrated, upset		испуганный	**26.** scared/afraid
сердитый	**19.** angry/mad		скучающий	**27.** bored
яростный	**20.** furious		гордый	**28.** proud
возмущённый	**21.** disgusted		смущённый	**29.** embarrassed
удивлённый	**22.** surprised		покрасневший	**30.** ashamed
шокированный	**23.** shocked		завистливый	**31.** jealous
нервный	**24.** nervous		сконфуженный	**32.** confused

A. Are you _____?
B. No. Why do you ask? Do I
   LOOK _____?
A. Yes. You do.

A. I'm _____.
B. Why?
A. ....

What makes you happy? sad? mad?
When do you feel nervous? annoyed?
Do you ever feel embarrassed? When?

[1–22]

A. This **apple** is delicious!
Where did you get it?
B. At *Shaw's Supermarket*.

[23–31]

A. These **grapes** are delicious!
Where did you get them?
B. At *Farmer Fred's Fruit Stand*.

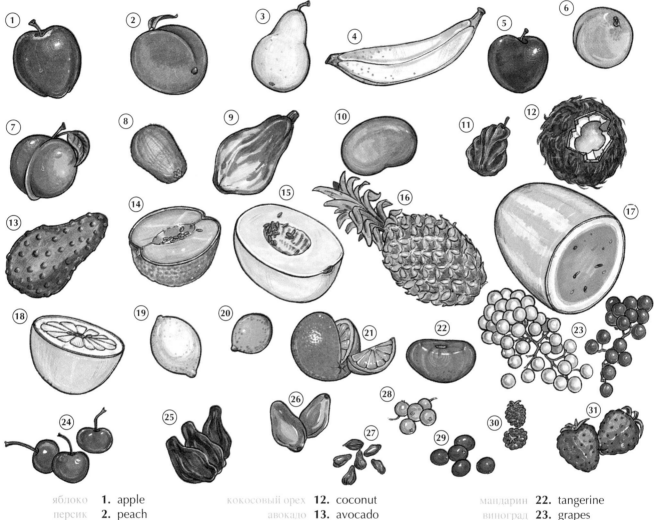

яблоко	**1.** apple	
персик	**2.** peach	
груша	**3.** pear	
банан	**4.** banana	
слива	**5.** plum	
абрикос	**6.** apricot	
нектарин	**7.** nectarine	
киви	**8.** kiwi	
папайя	**9.** papaya	
манго	**10.** mango	
инжир	**11.** fig	

кокосовый орех	**12.** coconut	
авокадо	**13.** avocado	
(мускусная) дыня	**14.** cantaloupe	
(мускатная) дыня	**15.** honeydew (melon)	
ананас	**16.** pineapple	
арбуз	**17.** watermelon	
грейпфрут	**18.** grapefruit	
лемон	**19.** lemon	
лайм	**20.** lime	
апельсин	**21.** orange	

мандарин	**22.** tangerine	
виноград	**23.** grapes	
вишня	**24.** cherries	
чернослив	**25.** prunes	
финики	**26.** dates	
изюм	**27.** raisins	
черника	**28.** blueberries	
клюква	**29.** cranberries	
малина	**30.** raspberries	
клубника	**31.** strawberries	

A. I'm hungry. Do we have any fruit?
B. Yes. We have _____s* and _____s.*

A. Do we have any more _____s?†
B. No. I'll get some more when I go to the supermarket.

What are your most favorite fruits?
What are your least favorite fruits?
Which of these fruits grow where you live?
Name and describe other fruits you are familiar with.

*With 14–18, use:
We have _____ and _____.

†With 14–18, use:
Do we have any more _____?

ОВОЩИ

A. What do we need from the supermarket?
B. We need **lettuce*** and **pea**s.†

*1–12   †13–36

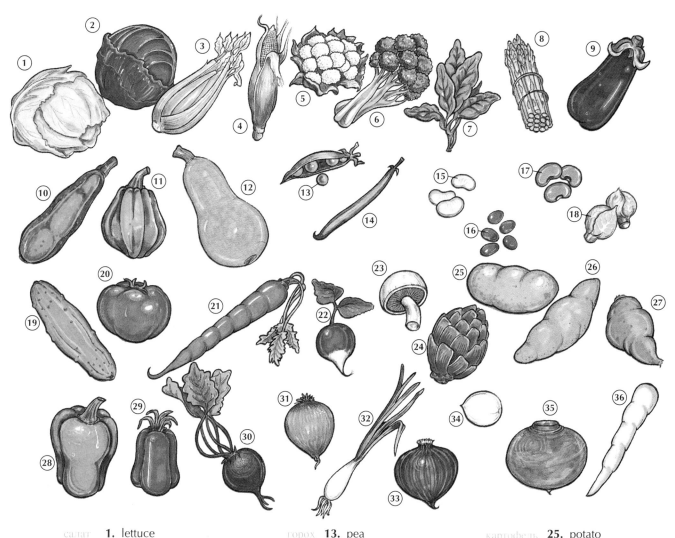

салат	**1.** lettuce	горох	**13.** pea	картофель	**25.** potato
капуста	**2.** cabbage	зелёная фасоль	**14.** string bean/	батат	**26.** sweet potato
сельдерей	**3.** celery		green bean	ямс/батат	**27.** yam
кукуруза	**4.** corn	зелёный боб	**15.** lima bean	зелёный перец	**28.** green pepper
цветная капуста	**5.** cauliflower	чёрный боб	**16.** black bean	красный перец	**29.** red pepper
брокколи/капуста	**6.** broccoli	фасоль	**17.** kidney bean	свёкла	**30.** beet
спаржевая		брюссельская капуста	**18.** brussels sprout	лук	**31.** onion
шпинат	**7.** spinach	огурец	**19.** cucumber	зелёный лук	**32.** scallion/
спаржа	**8.** asparagus	помидор	**20.** tomato		green onion
баклажан	**9.** eggplant	морковь	**21.** carrot	красный лук	**33.** red onion
зукини	**10.** zucchini (squash)	редиска	**22.** radish	жемчужный лук	**34.** pearl onion
кабачок	**11.** acorn squash	гриб	**23.** mushroom	репа/турнепс	**35.** turnip
кабачок	**12.** butternut squash	артишок	**24.** artichoke	пастернак	**36.** parsnip

A. How do you like the
  _[1–12]_ / _[13–36]_ s?
B. It's/They're delicious.

A. *Johnny?* Finish your vegetables!
B. But you KNOW I hate
  _[1–12]_ / _[13–36]_ s!
A. I know. But it's/they're good
  for you!

Which vegetables do you like?
Which vegetables don't you like?
Which of these vegetables grow where
  you live?
Name and describe other vegetables
  you are familiar with.

A. I'm going to the supermarket to get **milk** and **soup**.*
   Do we need anything else?
B. Yes. We also need **cereal** and **soda**.*

*With 43, 44, 46, 49, and 55, use: a _____.

Молочные продукты	**A. Dairy Products**
молоко	**1.** milk
нежирное молоко	**2.** low-fat milk
обезжиренное молоко	**3.** skim milk
шоколадное молоко	**4.** chocolate milk
пахта	**5.** buttermilk
апельсиновый сок	**6.** orange juice†
сыр	**7.** cheese
масло	**8.** butter
маргарин	**9.** margarine
сметана	**10.** sour cream
особая сметана	**11.** cream cheese
(прессованный) творог	**12.** cottage cheese
йогурт	**13.** yogurt
яйца	**14.** eggs

Консервированные продукты	**B. Canned Goods**
суп	**15.** soup
голубой тунец	**16.** tuna fish
консервированные овощи	**17.** (canned) vegetables
консервированные фрукты	**18.** (canned) fruit

Упакованные продукты	**C. Packaged Goods**
зерновые хлопья	**19.** cereal
печенье	**20.** cookies
сухое печенье	**21.** crackers
спагетти	**22.** spaghetti
лапша	**23.** noodles
макароны	**24.** macaroni
рис	**25.** rice

Сок	**D. Juice**
яблочный сок	**26.** apple juice
ананасовый сок	**27.** pineapple juice
грейпфрутовый сок	**28.** grapefruit juice
томатный сок	**29.** tomato juice
фруктовый пунш	**30.** fruit punch
виноградный сок	**31.** grape juice
клюквенный сок	**32.** cranberry juice
сок в пакетиках	**33.** juice paks
сок в порошке	**34.** powdered drink mix

Напитки	**E. Beverages**
газированная вода	**35.** soda
диетическая газировка	**36.** diet soda
бутылочная вода	**37.** bottled water

† Orange juice is not a dairy product, but is usually found in this section.

Птица	**F. Poultry**	сосиски/колбаски	54. sausages	мидия	67. clams
курица	38. chicken	ветчина/окорок	55. ham	крабы	68. crabs
куриные ляжки	39. chicken thighs	бекон	56. bacon	омар/морской рак	69. lobster
куриные ножки	40. drumsticks				
куриные грудки	41. chicken breasts	Морские продукты	**H. Seafood**	Выпечка	**I. Baked Goods**
куриные крылья	42. chicken wings	Рыба	FISH	английские булочки	70. English muffins
индюшка	43. turkey	лосось	57. salmon	торт/пирог	71. cake
утка	44. duck	палтус	58. halibut	пита/лепёшки	72. pita bread
		мелкая камбала	59. flounder	булочки	73. rolls
Мясо	**G. Meat**	меч-рыба	60. swordfish	хлеб	74. bread
фарш	45. ground beef	пикша	61. haddock		
жаркое	46. roast	форель	62. trout	Замороженные продукты	**J. Frozen Foods**
бифштекс	47. steak			мороженое	75. ice cream
мясо для тушки	48. stewing meat	Моллюски	SHELLFISH	замороженные овощи	76. frozen vegetables
баранья нога	49. leg of lamb	устрицы	63. oysters	замороженные ужины	77. frozen dinners
баранья отбивные	50. lamb chops	гребешки	64. scallops	замороженный лимонад	78. frozen lemonade
свинина	51. pork	креветки	65. shrimp	замороженный	79. frozen orange juice
свиные отбивные	52. pork chops	мидия	66. mussels	апельсиновый сок	
рёбра	53. ribs				

A. Excuse me. Where can I find
   _[1–79]_ ?
B. In the _[A–J]_ Section, next to
   the _[1–79]_ .
A. Thank you.

A. Pardon me. I'm looking for
   _[1–79]_ .
B. It's/They're in the _[A–J]_
   Section, between the
   _[1–79]_ and the _[1–79]_ .
A. Thanks.

Which of these foods do you like?
Which foods are good for you?
What brands of these foods do you
   buy?

УНИВЕРСАМ II

[1–70]

A. Look! _____ is/are on sale this week!

B. Let's get some!

Деликатесы	**A. Deli**
ростбиф	**1.** roast beef
колбаса "болонья"	**2.** bologna
салями	**3.** salami
ветчина	**4.** ham
индюшатина	**5.** turkey
солонина	**6.** corned beef
американский сыр	**7.** American cheese
швейцарский сыр	**8.** Swiss cheese
копчёный сыр	**9.** provolone
сыр "моццарелла"	**10.** mozzarella
чеддар	**11.** cheddar cheese
картофельный салат	**12.** potato salad
капустный салат	**13.** cole slaw
макаронный салат	**14.** macaroni salad
салат из морских	**15.** seafood salad
продуктов	

Закуски	**B. Snack Foods**
картошка ломтиками	**16.** potato chips
кукурузные чипсы	**17.** corn chips
тортилла чипсы	**18.** tortilla chips
начо чипсы	**19.** nacho chips
крендельки	**20.** pretzels
воздушная кукуруза	**21.** popcorn
орехи	**22.** nuts
земляные орехи/арахис	**23.** peanuts

Приправы	**C. Condiments**
кетчуп	**24.** ketchup
горчица	**25.** mustard
маринад	**26.** relish
солёные огурцы	**27.** pickles
маслины	**28.** black olives
соль	**29.** salt
перец	**30.** pepper
специи	**31.** spices

соевый соус	**32.** soy sauce
майонез	**33.** mayonnaise
масло	**34.** (cooking) oil
оливковое масло	**35.** olive oil
уксус	**36.** vinegar
салатная приправа	**37.** salad dressing

Кофе и чаи	**D. Coffee and Tea**
кофе	**38.** coffee
кофе без кофеина	**39.** decaffeinated coffee/
	decaf coffee
чай	**40.** tea
травяной чай	**41.** herbal tea
какао	**42.** cocoa/
	hot chocolate mix

Пекарные изделия	**E. Baking Products**
мука	**43.** flour
сахар	**44.** sugar
кекс	**45.** cake mix

Джемы и желе	**F. Jams and Jellies**	алюминиевая	**61.** aluminum foil	покупатель	**73.** shopper/customer
джем	**46.** jam	фольга		касса	**74.** checkout counter
желе	**47.** jelly	пластмассовая	**62.** plastic wrap	конвейер	**75.** conveyor belt
мармелад	**48.** marmalade	упаковка		купоны	**76.** coupons
арахисовая паста	**49.** peanut butter	восковая бумага	**63.** waxed paper	сканнер	**77.** scanner
				весы	**78.** scale
Бумажные товары	**G. Paper Products**	Детские продукты	**I. Baby Products**	касса	**79.** cash register
тонкая мягкая	**50.** tissues	детские хлопья	**64.** baby cereal	кассир	**80.** cashier
бумага		формула	**65.** formula	пластмассовый пакет	**81.** plastic bag
салфетки	**51.** napkins	детская питание	**66.** baby food	бумажный пакет	**82.** paper bag
туалетная бумага	**52.** toilet paper	мягкие салфетки	**67.** wipes	упаковщик	**83.** bagger/packer
бумажные	**53.** paper cups	одноразовые пелёнки	**68.** (disposable)	экспресс очередь	**84.** express checkout (line)
стаканчики			diapers	бульварная газета	**85.** tabloid (newspaper)
бумажные тарелки	**54.** paper plates			журнал	**86.** magazine
соломинки	**55.** straws	Продукты для	**J. Pet Food**	жевательная резинка	**87.** (chewing) gum
бумажные салфетки	**56.** paper towels	домашних животных		конфеты	**88.** candy
		корм для кошек	**69.** cat food	корзина для покупок	**89.** shopping basket
Хозяйственные товары	**H. Household Items**	корм для собак	**70.** dog food		
бутербродные пакеты	**57.** sandwich bags				
пакеты для мусора	**58.** trash bags	Место расчёта	**K. Checkout Area**		
мыло	**59.** soap	проход	**71.** aisle		
жидкое мыло	**60.** liquid soap	тележка для покупок	**72.** shopping cart		

A. Do we need [1–70] ?
B. No, but we need [1–70] .

A. We forgot to get [1–70] !
B. I'll get it/them.
   Where is it?/Where are they?
A. In the [A–J] Section over
   there.

Make a complete shopping list of
everything you need from the
supermarket.
Describe the differences between U.S.
supermarkets and food stores in
your country.

A. Would you please get a **bag** of *flour* when you go to the supermarket?
B. A **bag** of *flour?* Sure. I'd be happy to.

A. Would you please get two **head**s of *lettuce* when you go to the supermarket?
B. Two **head**s of *lettuce?* Sure. I'd be happy to.

пакет	**1.** bag	пучок/кисть/гроздь	**5.** bunch	дюжина	**9.** dozen*
кусок	**2.** bar	консервная банка	**6.** can	колос	**10.** ear
бутылка	**3.** bottle	картонный пакет	**7.** carton	кочан	**11.** head
коробка	**4.** box	коробка	**8.** container	банка	**12.** jar

* "a dozen eggs," NOT "a dozen of eggs."

буханка – буханки	**13.** loaf–loaves	налочка (масла)	**18.** stick	полгаллона	**22.** half-gallon
пачка	**14.** pack	кадка	**19.** tub	галлон	**23.** gallon
пакет	**15.** package	пинта	**20.** pint	литр	**24.** liter
рулон	**16.** roll	кварта	**21.** quart	фунт	**25.** pound
упаковка из шести	**17.** six-pack				

[At home]

A. What did you get at the supermarket?

B. I got _____, _____, and _____.

[In a supermarket]

A. Is this checkout counter open?

B. Yes, but this is the express line. Do you have more than eight items?

B. No. I only have _____, _____, and _____.

Open your kitchen cabinets and refrigerator. Make a list of all the things you find.

What do you do with empty bottles, jars, and cans? Do you recycle them, reuse them, or throw them away?

чайная ложка   столовая ложка   одна унция   чашка

teaspoon   tablespoon   1 (fluid) ounce   cup
tsp.   Tbsp.   1 fl. oz.   8 fl. ozs.

пинта   кварта   галлон

pint   quart   gallon
pt.   qt.   gal.
16 fl. ozs.   32 fl. ozs.   128 fl. ozs.

A. How much water should I put in?
B. The recipe says to add one _____ of water.

A. This fruit punch is delicious! What's in it?
B. Two _____s of orange juice, three _____s of grape juice, and a _____ of apple juice.

унция   четверть фунта   полфунта   три четверти фунта   фунт

an ounce   a quarter of a pound   half a pound   three-quarters of a pound   a pound
oz.   ¼ lb.   ½ lb.   ¾ lb.   lb.
     4 ozs.   8 ozs.   12 ozs.   16 ozs.

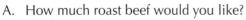

A. How much roast beef would you like?
B. I'd like _____, please.

A. This chili tastes very good! What did you put in it?
B. _____ of ground beef, _____ of beans, _____ of tomatoes, and _____ of chili powder.

A. Can I help?
B. Yes. Please **cut up** the *vegetables*.

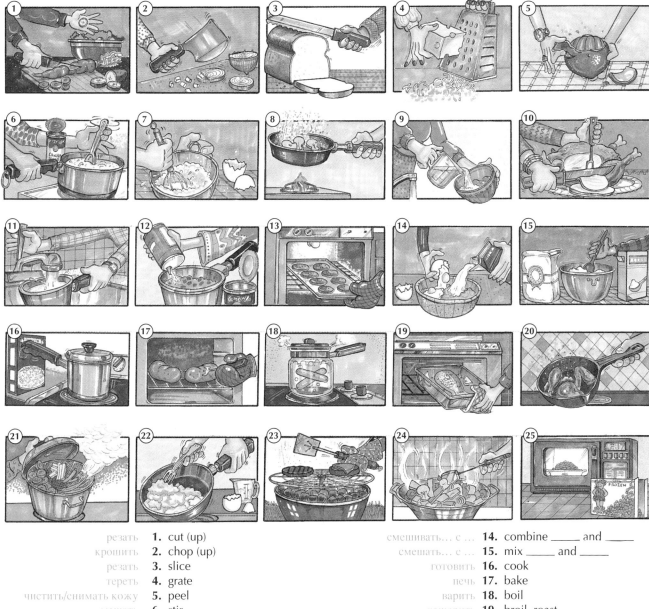

резать	**1.** cut (up)	смешивать… с …	**14.** combine _____ and _____
крошить	**2.** chop (up)	смешать… с …	**15.** mix _____ and _____
резать	**3.** slice	готовить	**16.** cook
тереть	**4.** grate	печь	**17.** bake
чистить/снимать кожу	**5.** peel	варить	**18.** boil
мешать	**6.** stir	зажарить	**19.** broil, roast
сбивать	**7.** beat	поджарить	**20.** fry
жарить	**8.** saute	парить	**21.** steam
лить	**9.** pour	взбалтывать	**22.** scramble
разделывать	**10.** carve	жарить на вертеле	**23.** barbecue/grill
наполнить	**11.** fill _____ with _____	помешивать	**24.** stir-fry
добавить… к …	**12.** add _____ to _____	готовить в микроволновой	**25.** microwave
положить… в …	**13.** put _____ in _____	печи	

[1–25] A. What are you doing?
       B. I'm _____ing the …………

[16–25] A. How long should I _____ the …………?
        B. For ……….. minutes/seconds.

What's your favorite recipe? Give instructions and use the units of measure on page 52. For example:

Mix a cup of flour and two tablespoons of sugar.
Add half a pound of butter.
Bake at 350° (degrees) for twenty minutes.

пончик	**1.** donut	диетическая кока-кола/пепси кола/севн-ап	**15.** Coke/Diet Coke/ Pepsi/7–Up/…	бутерброд с ростбифом	**26.** roast beef sandwich
кекс	**2.** muffin	лимонад	**16.** lemonade	бутерброд с солониной	**27.** corned beef sandwich
баранка/бублик	**3.** bagel	кофе	**17.** coffee	бутерброд с беконом, салатом и помидором	**28.** BLT/bacon, lettuce, and tomato sandwich
булочка	**4.** bun	кофе без кофеина	**18.** decaf coffee		
пирожное	**5.** danish/pastry	чай	**19.** tea		
бисквит	**6.** biscuit	чай со льдом	**20.** iced tea	белый хлеб	**29.** white bread
рогалик	**7.** croissant	молоко	**21.** milk	ржаной хлеб	**30.** rye bread
гамбургер	**8.** hamburger	бутерброд с тунцом	**22.** tuna fish sandwich	пшеничный хлеб	**31.** whole wheat bread
гамбургер с сыром	**9.** cheeseburger	бутерброд с яичным салатом	**23.** egg salad sandwich	немецкий ржаной хлеб	**32.** pumpernickel
сосиска	**10.** hot dog	бутерброд с куриным салатом	**24.** chicken salad sandwich	пита/лепёшка	**33.** pita bread
маисовая лепёшка с начинкой	**11.** taco			булочка	**34.** a roll
кусок пиццы	**12.** slice of pizza	бутерброд с ветчиной и сыром	**25.** ham and cheese sandwich	сабмарин (бутерброд)	**35.** a submarine roll
тарелка супа "чили"	**13.** bowl of chili				
жареная курица	**14.** order of fried chicken				

A. May I help you?
B. Yes. I'd like a/an [1–14] , please.
A. Anything to drink?
B. Yes. I'll have a small/medium-size/ large/extra-large [15–21] .

A. I'd like a [22–28] on [29–35] , please.
B. What do you want on it?
A. Lettuce/tomato/mayonnaise/mustard/…

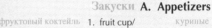
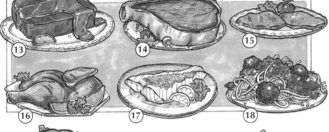

Закуски A. Appetizers

фруктовый коктейль	1. fruit cup/ fruit cocktail
томатный сок	2. tomato juice
креветочный коктейль	3. shrimp cocktail
куриные крылья	4. chicken wings
начоз	5. nachos
картофельная кожура	6. potato skins

Салаты B. Salads

овощной салат	7. tossed salad/ garden salad
греческий салат	8. Greek salad
шпинатовый салат	9. spinach salad
антипасто	10. antipasto
салат "Цезарь"	11. Caesar salad
салатный бар	12. salad bar

Основные/Главные блюда C. Main Courses/Entrees

мясной хлеб	13. meatloaf
ростбиф	14. roast beef/ prime rib
телячья котлета	15. veal cutlet
запечённая курица	16. baked chicken
жареная рыба	17. broiled fish
спагетти с фрикадельками	18. spaghetti and meatballs

Гарнир D. Side Dishes

печёный картофель	19. a baked potato
пюре	20. mashed potatoes
обжаренные картофельные стружки	21. french fries
рис	22. rice
лапша	23. noodles
овощи	24. mixed vegetables

Десерты E. Dessert

шоколадный торт	25. chocolate cake
яблочный пирог	26. apple pie
мороженое	27. ice cream
желе	28. jello
пудинг	29. pudding
мороженое сандей	30. ice cream sundae

[Ordering dinner]

A. May I take your order?
B. Yes, please. For the appetizer I'd like the [1–6].
A. And what kind of salad would you like?
B. I'll have the [7–12].
A. And for the main course?
B. I'd like the [13–18], please.
A. What side dish would you like with that?
B. Hmm. I think I'll have [19–24].

[Ordering dessert]
A. Would you care for some dessert?
B. Yes. I'll have [25–29] /an [30].

Do you go to restaurants? Which ones? What do you order? Describe some popular desserts in your country.

A. What's your favorite color?
B. **Red.**

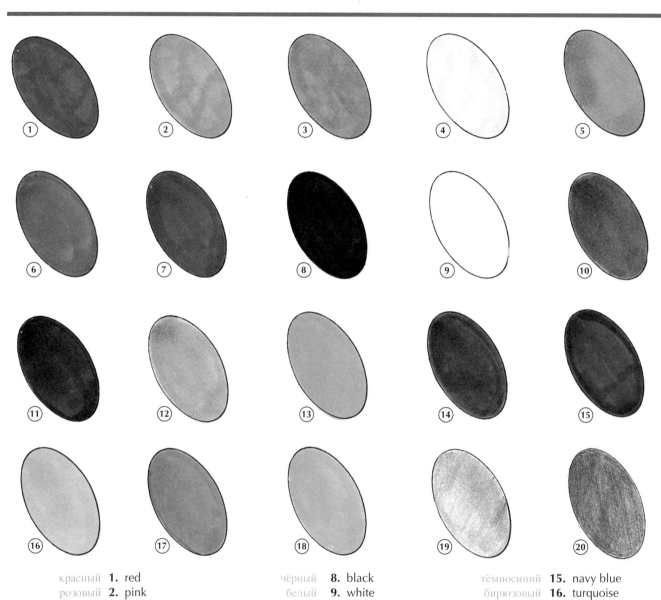

красный **1.** red	чёрный **8.** black	тёмносиний **15.** navy blue
розовый **2.** pink	белый **9.** white	бирюзовый **16.** turquoise
оранжевый **3.** orange	серый **10.** gray	тёмнорозовый **17.** hot pink
жёлтый **4.** yellow	коричневый **11.** brown	неоновозелёный **18.** neon green
зелёный **5.** green	бежевый **12.** beige	серебряный **19.** silver
синий/голубой **6.** blue	светлозелёный **13.** light green	золотой **20.** gold
пурпурный **7.** purple	тёмнозелёный **14.** dark green	

A. I like your _____ shirt.
You look very good in _____.
B. Thank you. _____ is my favorite
color.

A. My color TV is broken.
B. What's the matter with it?
A. People's faces are _____,
the sky is _____, and the
grass is _____!

Do you know the flags of different
countries? What are the colors of
the flags you know?
What color makes you happy? What
color makes you sad? Why?

ОДЕЖДА

A. I think I'll wear my new **shirt** today.
B. Good idea!

рубашка	**1.** shirt/long-sleeved	брюки	**9.** pants/slacks	форма	**20.** uniform
рубашка с короткми рукавом	**2.** short-sleeved shirt	голубые джинсы	**10.** (blue) jeans	пиджак	**21.** jacket/sports jacket/ sports coat
выходная рубашка	**3.** dress shirt	вельветовые брюки	**11.** corduroy pants/ corduroys	жакет	**22.** jacket
спортивная рубашка	**4.** sport shirt	юбка	**12.** skirt	блейзер	**23.** blazer
джерси	**5.** polo shirt/jersey/ sport shirt	платье	**13.** dress	костюм	**24.** suit
		комбинезон	**14.** jumpsuit	костюм – тройка	**25.** three-piece suit
		шорты	**15.** shorts	жилет	**26.** vest
фланелевая рубашка	**6.** flannel shirt	свитер	**16.** sweater	галстук	**27.** tie/necktie
блузка	**7.** blouse	свитер с разрезом	**17.** V-neck sweater	галстук – бабочка	**28.** bowtie
водолазка	**8.** turtleneck	кофта	**18.** cardigan sweater	смокинг	**29.** tuxedo
		комбинезон с помочами	**19.** overalls	вечернее платье	**30.** (evening) gown

пижама	**1.** pajamas	
ночной халат	**2.** nightgown	
ночная рубашка	**3.** nightshirt	
халат	**4.** bathrobe/robe	
тапочки	**5.** slippers	
нижняя майка	**6.** undershirt/ tee shirt	
трусы	**7.** (jockey) shorts/ underpants	
длинные трусы	**8.** boxer shorts	
суспензорий	**9.** athletic supporter/ jockstrap	
длинное нижнее бельё	**10.** long underwear/ long johns	

трусики	**11.** (bikini) panties/ underpants	
длинные трусики	**12.** briefs	
бюстгальтер	**13.** bra	
камзол	**14.** camisole	
нижняя сорочка	**15.** slip	
короткая комбинация	**16.** half slip	
чулки	**17.** stockings	
колготки	**18.** pantyhose	
колготки	**19.** tights	
носки	**20.** socks	
подколенники	**21.** knee socks	
ботинки/туфли	**22.** shoes	
туфли на высоком каблуке	**23.** (high) heels	

туфли	**24.** pumps
туфли	**25.** loafers
кроссовки	**26.** sneakers
теннисные кроссовки	**27.** tennis shoes
беговые кроссовки	**28.** running shoes
баскетбольные	**29.** high tops/ high-top sneakers
кроссовки	
сандалии	**30.** sandals
вьетнамки/"вьетнамки"	**31.** thongs/flip-flops
сапожки/ботинки	**32.** boots
рабочие ботинки	**33.** work boots
походные ботинки	**34.** hiking boots
ковбойские ботинки	**35.** cowboy boots
мокасины	**36.** moccasins

[1–21] A. I can't find my new _____.
B. Did you look in the bureau/dresser/closet?
A. Yes, I did.
B. Then it's/they're probably in the wash.

[22–36] A. Are those new _____?
B. Yes, they are.
A. They're very nice.
B. Thanks.

футболка	**1.** tee shirt	потничок	**11.** sweatband	галоши	**24.** rubbers
майка	**2.** tank top	пальто	**12.** coat	перчатки	**25.** gloves
хлопчатобумажный	**3.** sweatshirt	пальто	**13.** overcoat	варежки	**26.** mittens
свитер		куртка/жакет	**14.** jacket	шляпа	**27.** hat
хлопчатобумажные	**4.** sweat pants	ветровка	**15.** windbreaker	кепка	**28.** cap
штаны		лыжная куртка	**16.** ski jacket	бейсбольная шапочка	**29.** baseball cap
беговые шорты	**5.** running shorts	пилотская куртка	**17.** bomber jacket	берет	**30.** beret
теннисные шорты	**6.** tennis shorts	парка	**18.** parka	дождевая шляпа	**31.** rain hat
облегающие шорты	**7.** lycra shorts	пуховая куртка	**19.** down jacket	лыжная шапка	**32.** ski hat
беговой костюм	**8.** jogging suit/	пуховой жилет	**20.** down vest	лыжная маска	**33.** ski mask
	running suit	дождевая куртка	**21.** raincoat	муфты	**34.** ear muffs
леотард/трико	**9.** leotard	дождевая накидка	**22.** poncho	шарф	**35.** scarf
длинное трико	**10.** tights	плащ	**23.** trenchcoat		

[1–11]

A. Excuse me. I found this/these _____ in the dryer. Is it/Are they yours?

B. Yes. It's/They're mine. Thank you.

[12–35]

A. What's the weather like today?

B. It's cool/cold/raining/snowing.

A. I think I'll wear my _____.

ЮВЕЛИРНЫЕ ИЗДЕЛИЯ И АКСЕССУАРЫ

A. Oh, no! I think I lost my **ring**!
B. I'll help you look for it.

A. Oh, no! I think I lost my **earrings**!
B. I'll help you look for them.

перстень/кольцо	**1.** ring	булавка для галстука	**13.** tie pin/tie tack
обручальное кольцо	**2.** engagement ring	булавка для галстука	**14.** tie clip
обручальное кольцо	**3.** wedding ring/wedding band	ремень	**15.** belt
серьги	**4.** earrings	кольцо для ключей	**16.** key ring/key chain
ожерелье	**5.** necklace	кошелёк	**17.** wallet
жемчужное ожерелье	**6.** pearl necklace/pearls	кошелёк для мелочи	**18.** change purse
цепочка	**7.** chain	дамская сумочка	**19.** pocketbook/purse/handbag
бусы	**8.** beads	сумочка	**20.** shoulder bag
заколка	**9.** pin	сумка	**21.** tote bag
часы	**10.** watch/wrist watch	сумка для книг	**22.** book bag
браслет	**11.** bracelet	рюкзак	**23.** backpack
запонки	**12.** cuff links	портфель	**24.** briefcase
		зонт	**25.** umbrella

[In a store]
A. Excuse me. Is this/Are these _____ on sale this week?
B. Yes. It's/They're half price.

[On the street]
A. Help! Police! Stop that man/woman!
B. What happened?!
A. He/She just stole my _____ and my _____!

Do you like to wear jewelry? What jewelry do you have?
In your country, what do men, women, and children use to carry their things?

ОПИСАНИЕ ОДЕЖДЫ

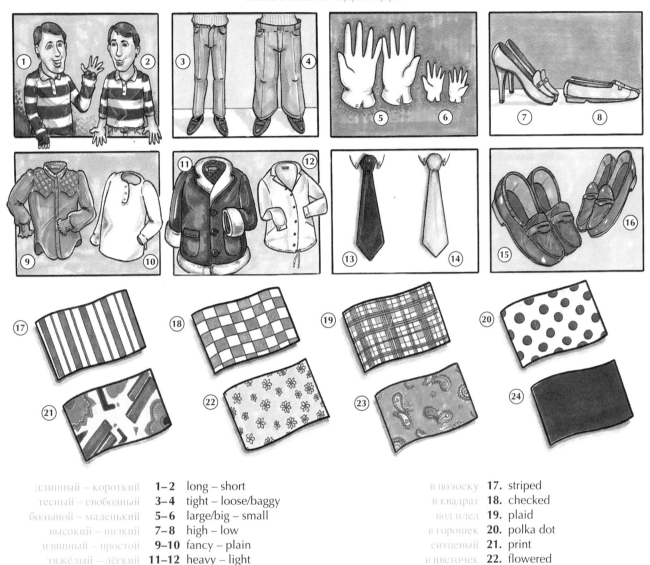

длинный – короткий	**1–2** long – short	в полоску	**17.** striped
тесный – свободный	**3–4** tight – loose/baggy	в квадрат	**18.** checked
большой – маленький	**5–6** large/big – small	под плед	**19.** plaid
высокий – низкий	**7–8** high – low	в горошек	**20.** polka dot
изящный – простой	**9–10** fancy – plain	ситцевый	**21.** print
тяжёлый – лёгкий	**11–12** heavy – light	в цветочек	**22.** flowered
тёмный – светлый	**13–14** dark – light	под персидский ковёр	**23.** paisley
широкий – узкий	**15–16** wide – narrow	полностью синий	**24.** solid *blue*

[1–2]
A. Are the sleeves too **long**?
B. No. They're too **short**.

1–2	Are the sleeves too _____?
3–4	Are the pants too _____?
5–6	Are the gloves too _____?
7–8	Are the heels too _____?

9–10	Is the blouse too _____?
11–12	Is the coat too _____?
13–14	Is the color too _____?
15–16	Are the shoes too _____?

[17–24]
A. How do you like this _____ tie/shirt/skirt?
B. Actually, I prefer that _____ one.

Describe your favorite clothing.

УНИВЕРМАГ

A. Excuse me. Where's the **store directory**?
B. It's over there, next to the **escalator**.

справочник/указатель	**1.** (store) directory	хозяйственный отдел **13.** Housewares Department
эскалатор	**2.** escalator	мебельный отдел **14.** Furniture Department/Home Furnishings Department
отдел мужской одежды	**3.** Men's Clothing Department	
парфюмерия (прилавок)	**4.** Perfume Counter	отдел приборов **15.** Household Appliances Department
ювелирные изделия (прилавок)	**5.** Jewelry Counter	отдел электроники **16.** Electronics Department
лифт	**6.** elevator	прилавок помощи покупателям **17.** Customer Assistance Counter/ Customer Service Counter
мужской туалет	**7.** men's room	
женский туалет	**8.** ladies' room	закусочный бар **18.** snack bar
фонтан	**9.** water fountain	отдел подарочной упаковки **19.** Gift Wrap Counter
стоянка-гараж	**10.** parking garage	автостоянка **20.** parking lot
отдел женской одежды	**11.** Women's Clothing Department	место выдачи покупок **21.** customer pickup area
отдел детской одежды	**12.** Children's Clothing Department	

A. Pardon me. Is this the way to the _____?
B. Yes, it is./No, it isn't.

A. I'll meet you at/in/near/in front of the _____.
B. Okay. What time?
A. At *3:00.*

Describe a department store you know. Tell what is on each floor.

ВИДЕО И ЗВУКОВАЯ АППАРАТУРА

A. May I help you?
B. Yes, please. I'm looking for a **TV**.

телевизор	**1.** TV/television set	стереосистема	**13.** stereo system/sound system
дистанционное управление	**2.** remote control (unit)	магнитофон	**14.** tape recorder
видеомагнитофон	**3.** VCR/videocassette recorder	плейер	**15.** (personal) cassette player/Walkman
(пустая) видеокассета	**4.** (blank) videotape		
видеокассета	**5.** video/(video)tape	переносная стереосистема	**16.** portable stereo system/boom box
видеокамера	**6.** camcorder/video camera		
проигрыватель	**7.** turntable	звуковая кассета	**17.** (audio) tape/(audio) cassette
приставка	**8.** tape deck	компактный диск	**18.** CD/compact disc
плейер для компактных дисков	**9.** CD player/compact disc player	пластинка	**19.** record
усилитель	**10.** amplifier	наушники	**20.** set of headphones
настройка	**11.** tuner	радиопроёмник	**21.** radio
колонка/громкоговоритель	**12.** speaker	коротковолновое радио	**22.** shortwave radio
		радио с часами	**23.** clock radio

A. How do you like my _____?
B. It's great/fantastic/awesome!

A. Which company makes a good _____?
B. In my opinion, the best _____ is made by ....

What video and audio equipment do you have or want?
In your opinion, which brands are the best?

A. Can you recommend a good **computer**?*
B. Yes. This **computer** here is excellent.

*With 9, use: Can you recommend good _____?

компьютер	**1.** computer		факс машина	**15.** fax machine
экран/монитор	**2.** monitor		фотоаппарат	**16.** camera
дисковод	**3.** disk drive		объективы	**17.** zoom lens
клавиатура	**4.** keyboard		сумка для фотоаппарата	**18.** camera case
мышь	**5.** mouse		вспышка	**19.** flash attachment
принтер	**6.** printer		тренога	**20.** tripod
модем	**7.** modem		фотоплёнка	**21.** film
диск	**8.** (floppy) disk/diskette		проектор для слайдов	**22.** slide projector
программное обеспечение	**9.** (computer) software		киноэкран	**23.** (movie) screen
переносной компьютер	**10.** portable computer		электрическая пишущая машинка	**24.** electric typewriter
компьютер-блокнот	**11.** notebook computer		электронная пишущая машинка	**25.** electronic typewriter
телефон	**12.** telephone/phone		калькулятор	**26.** calculator
переносной телефон	**13.** portable phone/portable telephone		арифмометр	**27.** adding machine
			стабилизатор	**28.** voltage regulator
автоответчик	**14.** answering machine		адаптер/переходник	**29.** adapter

A. Excuse me. Do you sell
 _____s?†
B. Yes. We carry a complete line of
 _____s.†

†With 9 and 21, use the singular.

A. Which _____ is the best?
B. This one here. It's made by
 …………

Do you have a camera? What kind
 is it? What do you take pictures of?
Does anyone you know have an
 answering machine? When you
 call, what does the machine say?
How have computers changed the world?

МАГАЗИН ИГРУШЕК

A. Excuse me. I'm looking for (a/an) _____(s) for my *grandson*.*
B. Look in the next aisle.
A. Thank you.

* *grandson/granddaughter/...*

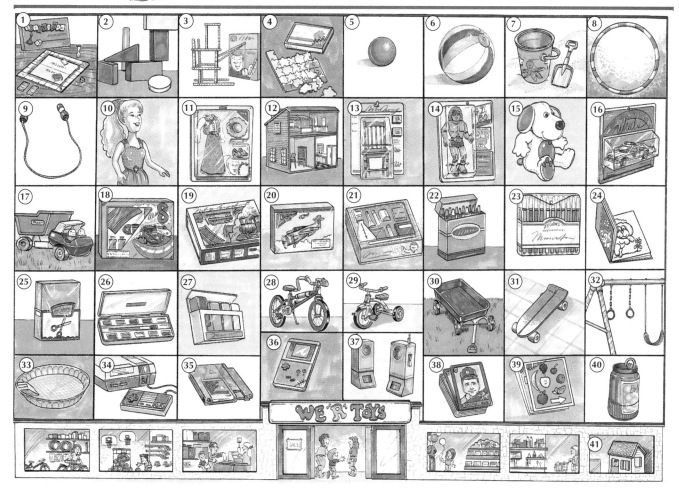

настольная игра	**1.** (board) game	грузовик	**17.** toy truck	скейтборд/доска на	**31.** skateboard
кубики	**2.** (building) blocks	набор гоночных	**18.** racing car	роликах	
конструктор	**3.** construction set	машин	set	качели	**32.** swing set
картинка-загадка	**4.** (jigsaw) puzzle	поезд (набор)	**19.** train set	и пластмассовый бассейн	**33.** plastic swimming
резиновый мяч	**5.** rubber ball	набор для	**20.** model kit		pool/wading pool
пляжный мяч	**6.** beach ball	моделирования		видеоигровая система	**34.** video game system
ведро и совок	**7.** pail and shovel	наука (набор)	**21.** science kit	видеоигровой диск	**35.** (video) game
обруч	**8.** hula hoop	цветные мелки	**22.** crayons		cartridge
прыгалки	**9.** jump rope	фломастер(ы)	**23.** (color) markers	ручная видеоигра	**36.** hand-held
кукла	**10.** doll	книжка для	**24.** coloring book		video game
одежда для куклы	**11.** doll clothing	раскрашивания		переговорное	**37.** walkie-talkie (set)
кукольный дом	**12.** doll house	набор цветной бумаги	**25.** construction paper	устройство (набор)	
мебель для	**13.** doll house	набор красок	**26.** paint set	карточки для обмена	**38.** trading cards
кукольного дома	furniture	пластилин	**27.** (modeling) clay	наклейки	**39.** stickers
персонаж из боевика	**14.** action figure	велосипед	**28.** bicycle	мыло для воздушных	**40.** bubble soap
игрушка	**15.** stuffed animal	трёхколёсный	**29.** tricycle	пузырей	
автомобиль со	**16.** matchbox car	велосипед		дом для игры	**41.** play house
спичечную коробку		тележка	**30.** wagon		

A. I don't know what to get my
............-year-old son/daughter
for his/her birthday.
B. What about (a) _____?

A. Mom/Dad? Can we buy
this/these _____?
B. No, *Johnny*. Not today.

What toys are most popular in your
country?
What were your favorite toys when
you were a child?

ДЕНЬГИ

Монеты / **Coins**

	Name	Value	Written as:	
1.	penny	one cent	1¢	$ .01
2.	nickel	five cents	5¢	$ .05
3.	dime	ten cents	10¢	$ .10
4.	quarter	twenty-five cents	25¢	$ .25
5.	half dollar	fifty cents	50¢	$ .50
6.	silver dollar	one dollar		$1.00

A. How much is a **penny** worth?
B. A penny is worth **one cent**.

A. *Soda* costs *seventy-five cents.*
   Do you have enough change?
B. Yes. I have a/two/three _____(s) and . . . .

Бумажные деньги / **Currency**

	Name	We sometimes say:	Value	Written as:
7.	(one-)dollar bill	a one	one dollar	$ 1.00
8.	five-dollar bill	a five	five dollars	$ 5.00
9.	ten-dollar bill	a ten	ten dollars	$ 10.00
10.	twenty-dollar bill	a twenty	twenty dollars	$ 20.00
11.	fifty-dollar bill	a fifty	fifty dollars	$ 50.00
12.	(one-)hundred dollar bill	a hundred	one hundred dollars	$100.00

A. I need to go to the supermarket.
   Do you have any cash?
B. Let me see. I have a **twenty-dollar bill**.
A. **Twenty dollars** is enough. Thanks.

A. Can you change a **five-dollar bill/a five**?
B. Yes. I've got *five* **one-dollar bills**/*five* **ones**.

Written as	We say:
$1.20	one dollar and twenty cents
	a dollar twenty
$2.50	two dollars and fifty cents
	two fifty
$37.43	thirty-seven dollars and forty-three cents
	thirty-seven forty-three

How much do you pay for a loaf of bread? a hamburger?
 a cup of coffee? a gallon of gas?
Name and describe the coins and currency in your country.
 What are they worth in U.S. dollars?

БАНК

чековая книжка	**1.** checkbook		чек	**10.** check
чековый реестр	**2.** check register		денежный перевод	**11.** money order
месячный баланс	**3.** monthly statement		заявление о займе	**12.** loan application
банковская книжка	**4.** bank book		банковский сейф	**13.** (bank) vault
аккредитивы	**5.** traveler's checks		ящик для ценных бумаг	**14.** safe deposit box
кредитная карточка	**6.** credit card		кассир	**15.** teller
карточка для кассы-автомата	**7.** ATM card		охрана	**16.** security guard
свидетельство о вкладе	**8.** deposit slip		автоматический кассовый	**17.** automatic teller (machine)/
свидетельство о снятии	**9.** withdrawal slip		аппарат	ATM (machine)
			работник банка	**18.** bank officer

[1–7]
A. What are you looking for?
B. My _____. I can't find it/them anywhere!

[8–12]
A. What are you doing?
B. I'm filling out this _____.
A. For how much?
B. ....

[13–18]
A. How many _____s does the State Street Bank have?
B. ....

Do you have a bank account? What kind? Where?
Do you ever use traveler's checks? When?
Do you have a credit card? What kind? When do you use it?

[1–23, 27–79]

A. My doctor checked my **head** and said everything is okay.
B. I'm glad to hear that.

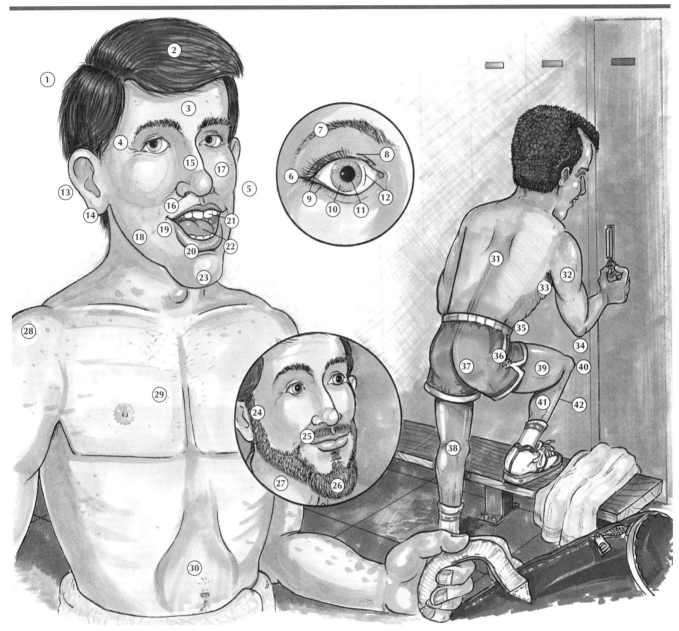

голова	**1.** head	нос	**15.** nose	грудь	**29.** chest
волосы	**2.** hair	ноздря	**16.** nostril	живот	**30.** abdomen
лоб	**3.** forehead	щека	**17.** cheek	спина	**31.** back
висок	**4.** temple	челюсть	**18.** jaw	рука	**32.** arm
лицо	**5.** face	рот	**19.** mouth	подмышка	**33.** armpit
глаз	**6.** eye	губа	**20.** lip	локоть	**34.** elbow
бровь	**7.** eyebrow	зуб – зубы	**21.** tooth–teeth	талия	**35.** waist
веко	**8.** eyelid	язык	**22.** tongue	бедро	**36.** hip
ресница	**9.** eyelashes	подбородок	**23.** chin	ягодицы	**37.** buttocks
радужная оболочка	**10.** iris	баки	**24.** sideburns	нога	**38.** leg
зрачок	**11.** pupil	усы	**25.** mustache	бедро	**39.** thigh
роговица	**12.** cornea	борода	**26.** beard	колено	**40.** knee
ухо	**13.** ear	шея	**27.** neck	икра	**41.** calf
мочка	**14.** earlobe	плечо	**28.** shoulder	голень	**42.** shin

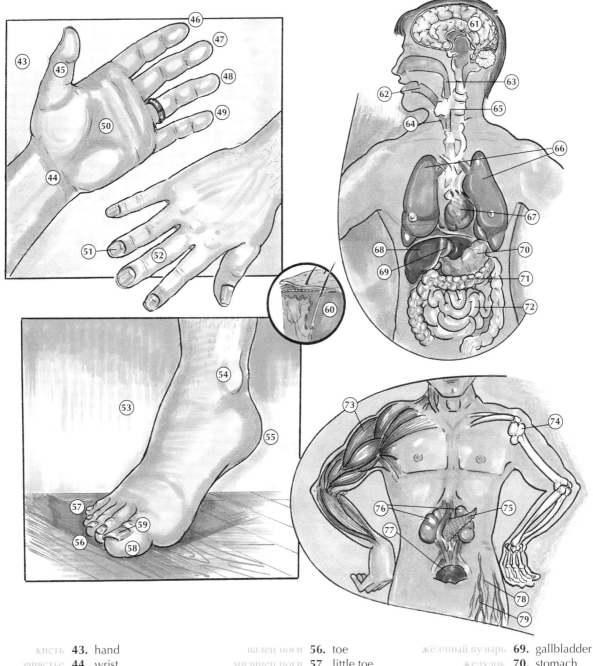

кисть	**43.** hand	палец ноги	**56.** toe	жёлчный пузырь	**69.** gallbladder
запястье	**44.** wrist	мизинец ноги	**57.** little toe	желудок	**70.** stomach
большой палец	**45.** thumb	большой палец ноги	**58.** big toe	толстая кишка	**71.** large intestine
указательный палец	**46.** (index) finger	ноготь	**59.** toenail	тонкая кишка	**72.** small intestine
средний палец	**47.** middle finger	кожа	**60.** skin	мышцы/мускулы	**73.** muscles
безымянный палец	**48.** ring finger	мозг	**61.** brain	кости	**74.** bones
мизинец	**49.** pinky/little finger	горло	**62.** throat	поджелудочная	**75.** pancreas
ладонь	**50.** palm	пищевод	**63.** esophagus	железа	
ноготь	**51.** fingernail	дыхательное горло	**64.** windpipe	почки	**76.** kidneys
сустав	**52.** knuckle	спинной мозг	**65.** spinal cord	мочевой пузырь	**77.** bladder
ступня	**53.** foot	лёгкие	**66.** lungs	вены	**78.** veins
лодыжка/щиколотка	**54.** ankle	сердце	**67.** heart	артерии	**79.** arteries
пятка	**55.** heel	печень	**68.** liver		

[1, 3–8, 13–23, 27–34, 36–60]

A. Ooh!

B. What's the matter?

A. { My _____ hurts!
 { My _____s hurt!

[61–79]

A. My doctor wants me to have some tests.

B. Why?

A. She's concerned about my _____.

Describe yourself as completely as you can.

Which parts of the body are most important at school? at work? when you play your favorite sport?

БОЛЕЗНИ, СИМПТОМЫ И ТРАВМЫ

A. What's the matter?
B. I have a/an [1–19] .

A. What's the matter?
B. I have [20–26] .

головная боль	**1.** headache	вирус	**10.** virus	бородавка	**19.** wart
ушная боль	**2.** earache	инфекция	**11.** infection	икота	**20.** (the) hiccups
зубная боль	**3.** toothache	сыпь	**12.** rash	озноб	**21.** (the) chills
боль в желудке	**4.** stomachache	укус насекомого	**13.** insect bite	спазмы	**22.** cramps
боль в спине	**5.** backache	солнечный ожог	**14.** sunburn	понос	**23.** diarrhea
больное горло	**6.** sore throat	(ему) надуло в шею	**15.** stiff neck	грудная боль	**24.** chest pain
жар/температура	**7.** fever/	насморк	**16.** runny nose	одышка	**25.** shortness of breath
	temperature	кровь из носа	**17.** bloody nose	ларингит	**26.** laryngitis
простуда	**8.** cold	дупло	**18.** cavity		
кашель	**9.** cough				

A. What's the matter?
B. { I feel _[27–30]_ .
    { I'm _[31–32]_ .
    { I'm _[33–38]_ ing.

A. What's the matter?
B. { I _[39–48]_ ed my ....
    { My .... is/are _[49–50]_ .

обморок	**27.** faint	сопеть/хрипеть	**35.** wheeze	оцарапать	**43.** scrape
головокружение	**28.** dizzy	рыгать	**36.** burp	поставить синяк/ушибить	**44.** bruise
(мне) тошнит	**29.** nauseous	рвать	**37.** vomit/throw up	обжечься	**45.** burn
раздутый	**30.** bloated	кровоточить	**38.** bleed	сломать	**46.** break–broke
заложило нос	**31.** congested	вывихнуть	**39.** twist	ушибить	**47.** hurt–hurt
измученный/изнурённый	**32.** exhausted	растянуть	**40.** sprain	порезать	**48.** cut–cut
кашлять	**33.** cough	вывихнуть	**41.** dislocate	распухший	**49.** swollen
чихать	**34.** sneeze	оцарапать	**42.** scratch	зудящий	**50.** itchy

A. How do you feel?
B. Not so good./Not very well./Terrible!
A. What's the matter?
B. ...., ..., and ....
A. I'm sorry to hear that.

Tell about the last time you didn't feel well. What was the matter?
Tell about a time you hurt yourself. What happened? How?
What are the symptoms of a cold? a heart problem?

доктор/врач	**1.** doctor/physician	кардиолог	**11.** cardiologist	перчатки	**21.** gloves

докто́р/врач | **1.** doctor/physician
медсестра́ | **2.** nurse
те́хник де́лающий | **3.** X-ray technician
рентгогра́ммы
лабора́нт | **4.** lab technician
рабо́тник ско́рой | **5.** EMT/emergency
по́мощи | medical technician
зубно́й врач | **6.** dentist
гигиени́ст | **7.** (oral) hygienist
акуше́р | **8.** obstetrician
гинеко́лог | **9.** gynecologist
педиа́тр | **10.** pediatrician

кардио́лог | **11.** cardiologist
глазно́й врач | **12.** optometrist
хиру́рг | **13.** surgeon
психиа́тр | **14.** psychiatrist
экзаменацио́нный | **15.** examination table
стол
(глазна́я) табли́ца | **16.** eye chart
весы́ | **17.** scale
рентге́новский | **18.** X-ray machine
аппара́т
стетоско́п | **19.** stethoscope
гра́дусник | **20.** thermometer

перча́тки | **21.** gloves
прибо́р для | **22.** blood pressure gauge
измере́ния
давле́ния
шприц | **23.** needle/syringe
повя́зка | **24.** bandages/gauze
кле́йкая ле́нта | **25.** adhesive tape
спирт | **26.** alcohol
ва́тные ша́рики | **27.** cotton balls
сверло́/бур | **28.** drill
новока́ин | **29.** anesthetic/
Novocaine

[1–14]
A. What do you do?
B. I'm a/an _____.

[15–18]
A. Please step over here to the _____.
B. Okay.

[19–29]
A. Please hand me the _____.
B. Here you are.

Where do you go for medical care? How often? Who examines you? What does he/she do?

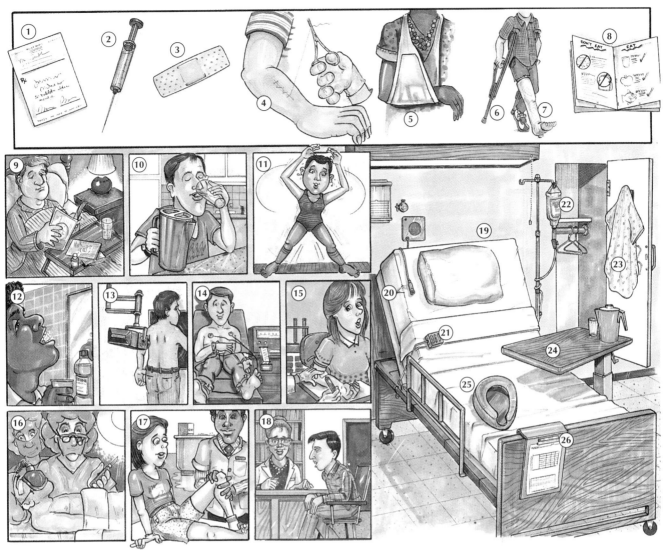

рецепт	**1.** prescription	делать упражнения	**11.** exercise	больничная кровать	**19.** hospital bed
укол	**2.** injection/shot	полоскать горло	**12.** gargle	кнопка для вызова	**20.** call button
(клейкая) повязка	**3.** bandaid	рентгеновские	**13** X-rays	контроль постели	**21.** bed control
швы	**4.** stitches	снимки/рентгенограммы		внутривенное	**22.** I.V.
повязка	**5.** sling	анализы	**14.** tests	устройство	
костыли	**6.** crutches	анализ крови	**15.** blood work/	больничный халат	**23.** hospital gown
гипс	**7.** cast		blood tests	столик у кровати	**24.** bed table
диета	**8.** diet	операция	**16.** surgery	судно	**25.** bed pan
отдыхать в постели	**9.** rest in bed	физическая терапия	**17.** physical therapy	медицинская карта	**26.** medical chart
пить жидкости	**10.** drink fluids	консультация	**18.** counseling		

[1–8]
A. What did the doctor do?
B. She/He gave me (a/an) _____ .

[9–18]
A. What did the doctor say?
B. { She/He told me to [9–12] .
{ She/He told me I need [13–18] .

[19–26]
A. This is your _____ .
B. I see.

When did you have your last medical checkup?
What did the doctor say?

Have you ever been in the hospital?
When? Why? Tell about your experience.

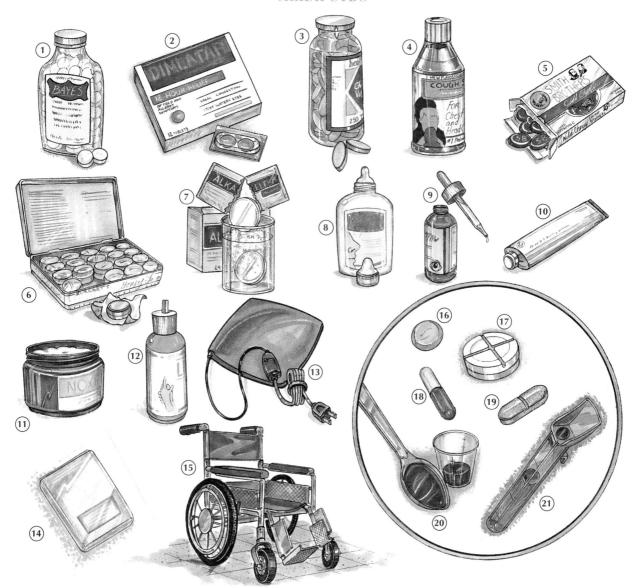

аспирин	**1.** aspirin
таблетки от простуды	**2.** cold tablets
витамины	**3.** vitamins
сироп от кашля	**4.** cough syrup
леденцы от кашля	**5.** cough drops
таблетки от горла	**6.** throat lozenges
антикислотные таблетки	**7.** antacid tablets

капли в нос	**8.** decongestant spray/nasal spray
глазные капли	**9.** eye drops
мазь	**10.** ointment
крем	**11.** creme
лосьон	**12.** lotion
грелка	**13.** heating pad
пузырь со льдом	**14.** ice pack

инвалидная коляска	**15.** wheelchair
пилюля	**16.** pill
таблетка	**17.** tablet
капсула	**18.** capsule
продолговатая таблетка	**19.** caplet
чайная ложка	**20.** teaspoon
столовая ложка	**21.** tablespoon

[1–15]   A. What did the doctor say?

B. { She/He told me to take [1–4] .
{ She/He told me to use (a/an) [5–15] .

[16–21]   A. What's the dosage?
            B. One _____, every three hours.

What medicines do you take or use?
For what ailments?

Describe any medical treatments or medicines in your
country that are different from the ones in these lessons.

ПОЧТА

письмо	**1.** letter	марка	**11.** stamp	марка
почтовая открытка	**2.** postcard	лист марок	**12.** sheet of stamps	почтовый штемпель
авиаписьмо	**3.** air letter/ aerogramme	марочный рулон	**13.** roll of stamps	отверстие для
посылка	**4.** package/parcel	буклет марок	**14.** book of stamps	опускания почты
первый класс	**5.** first class	денежный перевод	**15.** money order	окошко
авиа	**6.** air mail	бланк "Смена адреса"	**16.** change-of-address form	работник почты
почтово-посылочная служба	**7.** parcel post	бланк для регистрации	**17.** selective service registration form	весы
третий класс	**8.** book rate/third class	воинской повинности		автомат по продаже марок
заказная почта	**9.** registered mail	конверт	**18.** envelope	почтовый грузовик
экспресс почта	**10.** express mail/ overnight mail	адрес	**19.** address	почтовый ящик
		почтовый индекс	**20.** zip code	почтальон
		обратный адрес	**21.** return address	почтовая сумка

22. stamp/postage	
23. postmark	
24. mail slot	
25. window	
26. postal worker/ postal clerk	
27. scale	
28. stamp machine	
29. mail truck	
30. mailbox	
31. letter carrier/ mail carrier	
32. mail bag	

[1–4]
A. Where are you going?
B. To the post office.
   I have to mail a/an _____.

[5–10]
A. How do you want to send it?
B. _____, please.

[11–17]
A. Next!
B. I'd like a _____, please.
A. Here you are.

[19–22]
A. Do you want me to mail this letter for you?
B. Yes, thanks.
A. Oops! You forgot the _____!

What time does your letter carrier deliver your mail? Does he/she drive a mail truck or carry a mail bag and walk?

Describe the post office you use:
How many postal windows are there?
Is there a stamp machine?
Are the postal workers friendly?

Tell about the postal system in your country.

библиотекарь	**1.** librarian	работник	**11.** reference librarian	газета **22.** newspaper
стол	**2.** checkout desk	справочного отдела		журнал **23.** magazine
регистрации книг		справочный отдел	**12.** reference section	(научный) журнал **24.** journal
ассистент	**3.** library assistant	атлас	**13.** atlas	каталожная карточка **25.** call card
микрофильм	**4.** microfilm	энциклопедия	**14.** encyclopedia	шифр **26.** call number
микрофиша	**5.** microfiche	словарь	**15.** dictionary	автор **27.** author
карточный	**6.** card catalog	информационный	**16.** media section	название **28.** title
каталог		отдел		предмет/тема **29.** subject
компьютер-каталог	**7.** online catalog	видеокассета	**17.** videotape	библиотечная карточка **30.** library card
полки	**8.** shelves	пластинка	**18.** record	
информация	**9.** information desk	кассета	**19.** tape	
копировальное	**10.** copier/(photo)	компьютерный диск	**20.** computer diskette	
устройство	copy machine	отдел периодики	**21.** periodicals section	

[1–11]

A. Excuse me. Where's/ Where are the _____?

B. Over there, at/near/next to the _____.

[12–24]

A. Excuse me. Where can I find a/an [13–15, 17–20, 22–24] ?

B. Look in the [12, 16, 21] over there.

[27–29]

A. May I help you?

B. Yes, please. I'm having trouble finding a book.

A. Do you know the _____?

B. Yes. …………

Do you go to a library? Which one? What does this library have? Describe how you use the library.

кабинет/канцелярия	**1.** office	лингафонный	**8.** language lab	беговая дорожка/трек	**16.** track
медпункт	**2.** nurse's office	кабинет		директор	**17.** principal
кабинет советника	**3.** guidance office	химическая	**9.** chemistry lab	завуч	**18.** assistant principal
кафетерий/столовая	**4.** cafeteria	лаборатория		медсестра	**19.** (school) nurse
директорский	**5.** principal's	учительская (комната)	**10.** teachers' lounge	советник	**20.** guidance counselor
кабинет	office	гимнастический зал	**11.** gym/gymnasium	дежурный по столовой	**21.** lunchroom monitor
классная	**6.** classroom	раздевалка	**12.** locker room	работник столовой	**22.** cafeteria worker
комната/класс		зрительный зал	**13.** auditorium	водитель-инструктор	**23.** driver's ed instructor
шкаф с замком	**7.** locker	поле	**14.** field	учитель	**24.** teacher
		трибуны (стадиона)	**15.** bleachers	тренер	**25.** coach
				технический работник	**26.** custodian

[1–16] A. Where are you going?
B. I'm going to the _____.*
A. Do you have a hall pass?
B. Yes. Here it is.

With 6 and 7, use: I'm going to my _____.

[17–26] A. Who's that?
B. That's the new

Describe the school where you study English.
Tell about the rooms, offices, and people.

Tell about differences between schools in the United States
and in your country.

  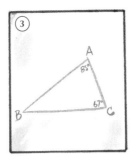  

  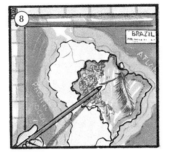 

  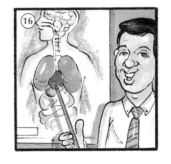 

математика	**1.** math/mathematics	география	**8.** geography	внутренняя экономика	**15.** home economics
алгебра	**2.** algebra	наука	**9.** science	здоровье	**16.** health
геометрия	**3.** geometry	биология	**10.** biology	труд	**17.** industrial arts/shop
тригонометрия	**4.** trigonometry	химия	**11.** chemistry	вождение	**18.** driver's education/ driver's ed
вычислительная математика	**5.** calculus	физика	**12.** physics		
английский язык	**6.** English	испанский язык	**13.** Spanish	машинопись	**19.** typing
история	**7.** history	французский язык	**14.** French	изобразительное искусство	**20.** art
				музыка	**21.** music

(духовой) оркестр	**22.**	band
оркестр	**23.**	orchestra
хор	**24.**	choir/chorus
драма	**25.**	drama
американский футбол	**26.**	football

школьная газета	**27.**	school newspaper
годовая книга	**28.**	yearbook
литературный журнал	**29.**	literary magazine
студенческое самоуправление	**30.**	student government

[1–21]
A. What do you have next period?
B. _____. How about you?
A. _____.
B. There's the bell. I've got to go.

[22–30]
A. Are you going home right after school?
B. { No. I have [22–26] practice.
    { No. I have a [27–30] meeting.

What is/was your favorite subject? Why? What extracurricular activities do/did you participate in?

СПЕЦИАЛЬНОСТИ I

A. What do you do?
B. I'm an **accountant**. How about you?
A. I'm a **carpenter**.

бухгалтер	**1.** accountant	сборщик	**6.** assembler	водитель автобуса	**11.** bus driver
актёр	**2.** actor	пекарь	**7.** baker	мясник	**12.** butcher
актриса	**3.** actress	парикмахер	**8.** barber	плотник	**13.** carpenter
архитектор	**4.** architect	счетовод	**9.** bookkeeper	кассир	**14.** cashier
художник	**5.** artist	каменщик	**10.** bricklayer/mason	повар/шеф	**15.** chef/cook

компьютерный программист	**16.** computer programmer	обрабатывающий информацию	**20.** data processor	рыбак	**25.** fisherman
строитель	**17.** construction worker	разносчик	**21.** delivery person	мастер	**26.** foreman
курьер	**18.** courier/messenger	электрик	**22.** electrician	садовник	**27.** gardener
технический работник	**19.** custodian/janitor	фермер	**23.** farmer	парикмахерша	**28.** hairdresser
		пожарник	**24.** firefighter	домохозяйка	**29.** housekeeper
				журналист/репортёр	**30.** journalist/reporter

[At a job interview]
A. Are you an experienced _____?
B. Yes. I'm a very experienced _____.

A. How long have you been a/an _____?
B. I've been a/an _____ for .... months/years.

Which of these occupations do you think are the most interesting? the most difficult? Why?

СПЕЦИАЛЬНОСТИ II

A. What's your occupation?
B. I'm a **lawyer**.
A. A **lawyer**?
B. Yes. That's right.

юрист	**1.** lawyer	фотограф	**7.** photographer	секретарь по приёму посетителей	**12.** receptionist
механик	**2.** mechanic	пилот	**8.** pilot		
натурщица	**3.** model	водопроводчик	**9.** plumber	ремонтник	**13.** repairperson
диктор новостей	**4.** newscaster	милиционер	**10.** police officer	продавец	**14.** salesperson
маляр	**5.** painter	агент по продаже домов	**11.** real estate agent	мусорщик	**15.** sanitation worker
аптекарь	**6.** pharmacist				

учёный	**16.** scientist	портной	**21.** tailor	водитель грузовика **26.** truck driver
швея	**17.** seamstress	таксист	**22.** taxi driver	официант **27.** waiter
секретарь	**18.** secretary	учитель/преподаватель	**23.** teacher	официантка **28.** waitress
сторож	**19.** security guard	переводчик	**24.** translator/interpreter	сварщик **29.** welder
снабженец	**20.** stock clerk	агент бюро путешествий	**25.** travel agent	ветеринар **30.** veterinarian

A. Are you still a _____?
B. No. I'm a _____.
A. Oh. That's interesting.

A. What kind of job would you like in the future?
B. I'd like to be a _____.

Do you work? What's your occupation?
What are the occupations of people in your family?

ВИДЫ ДЕЯТЕЛЬНОСТИ

A. Can you **act**?
B. Yes, I can.

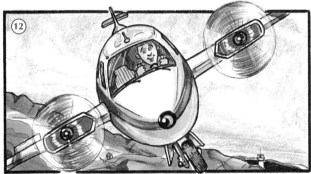

играть	**1.** act	чистить	**5.** clean	водить *грузовик*	**10.** drive *a truck*
работать на	**2.** assemble *components*	готовить	**6.** cook	регистрировать	**11.** file
конвейере		разносить *пищу*	**7.** deliver *pizzas*	летать *на самолёте*	**12.** fly *an airplane*
печь	**3.** bake	проектировать	**8.** design *buildings*	выращивать *овощи*	**13.** grow *vegetables*
строить	**4.** build *things/*	рисовать/чертить	**9.** draw	охранять *здания*	**14.** guard *buildings*
	construct *things*				

косить *газоны*	**15.** mow *lawns*	шить	**22.** sew
работать на станке	**16.** operate *equipment*	петь	**23.** sing
красить	**17.** paint	преподавать/учить	**24.** teach
играть на *рояле*	**18.** play the *piano*	переводить	**25.** translate
чинить/ремонтировать	**19.** repair *things*/fix *things*	печатать на машинке	**26.** type
продавать *автомобили*	**20.** sell *cars*	мыть *посуду*	**27.** wash *dishes*
обслуживать	**21.** serve *food*	писать	**28.** write

A. What do you do for a living?
B. I _____.

A. Do you know how to _____?
B. Yes. I've been _____ing for years.

Tell about your work abilities.
What can you do?

УЧРЕЖДЕНИЕ/КОНТОПА/КАНЦЕЛЯРИЯ/КАБИНЕТ

приёмная	**1.** reception area
вешалка для одежды	**2.** coat rack
шкаф для одежды	**3.** coat closet
доска объявлений	**4.** message board
почтовый ящик	**5.** mailbox
шкаф для папок/дел	**6.** file cabinet
шкаф для канцелярских принадлежностей	**7.** supply cabinet
шкаф для хранения	**8.** storage cabinet
рабочее место	**9.** workstation
рабочее место с компьютером	**10.** computer workstation
охладитель воды	**11.** water cooler
кофейный столик	**12.** coffee cart
кабинет	**13.** office
почтовая комната	**14.** mailroom
почтовая машина	**15.** postage machine/postage meter
копировальное устройство	**16.** copier/(photo)copy machine

ящик для мусора	**17.** waste receptacle
комната для канцелярских товаров	**18.** supply room
комната для хранения	**19.** storage room
зал заседаний	**20.** conference room
конференционный стол	**21.** conference table
белая доска	**22.** whiteboard/dry erase board
комната отдыха для работников	**23.** employee lounge
кофейный аппарат	**24.** coffee machine
автомат с газированной водой	**25.** soda machine
секретарь по приёму посетителей	**26.** receptionist
машинистка	**27.** typist
регистратор	**28.** file clerk
секретарь	**29.** secretary
помощник	**30.** administrative assistant
менеджер/управляющий учреждения/конторы	**31.** office manager
ассистент	**32.** office assistant
босс/начальник/управляющий	**33.** employer/boss

[1–25]   A.   Where's ....?

B   He's/She's in the/his/her _____.*
     He's/She's at the/his/her _____.†

*1, 13, 14, 18–20, 23   †2–12, 15–17, 21, 22, 24, 25

[26–33]   A.   Who's he/she?

          B.   He's/She's the new _____.

ОБОРУДОВАНИЕ В УЧРЕЖДЕНИИ/КОНТОРЕ

A. Do you know how to work this **computer**?
B. No, I don't.
A. Let me show you how.

компьютер	**1.** computer	пишущая машинка	**7.** typewriter	факс машина	**15.** fax machine
видеомонитор	**2.** VDT/video display terminal	калькулятор	**8.** calculator	точилка для карандашей	**16.** pencil sharpener
принтер	**3.** (dot-matrix) printer	арифмометр	**9.** adding machine	электроточилка для	**17.** electric pencil sharpener
принтер (с более	**4.** (letter-quality) printer	диктофон	**10.** microcassette recorder/ dictaphone	карандашей	
качественным				резак для бумаги	**18.** paper cutter
шрифтом)		телефон	**11.** telephone	переплётная машина	**19.** plastic binding machine
лазерный принтер	**5.** (laser) printer	наушники	**12.** headset	почтовые весы	**20.** postal scale
электронный	**6.** word processor	с микрофоном		бумажный дезинтегратор	**21.** paper shredder
печатающий		телефонная система	**13.** phone system		
аппарат		телекс	**14.** telex machine		

A. I think this _____ is broken!
B. I'll take a look at it.

A. Have you seen the new _____?
B. No, I haven't.
A. It's much better than the old one!

Do you know how to operate a computer? a fax machine? Give step-by-step instructions for using some type of office equipment.

ОБСТАНОВКА В КАБИНЕТЕ

стол	**1.** desk	настенный календарь	**13.** wall calendar
вращающееся кресло	**2.** swivel chair	расписание	**14.** wall planner
карточки с адресами	**3.** rolodex	шкаф для папок/дел	**15.** file cabinet
стакан для карандашей	**4.** pencil cup	скоросшиватель	**16.** stapler
поднос для писем	**5.** letter tray/ stacking tray	скобкоудалитель	**17.** staple remover
		раздаточное устройство для ленты	**18.** tape dispenser
подставка для записок	**6.** memo holder	раздаточное устройство для скрепок	**19.** paper clip dispenser
настольный календарь	**7.** desk calendar	бизнес-карточки	**20.** business cards
		доска с зажимом	**21.** clipboard
настольная лампа	**8.** desk lamp	книга приёмов и встреч	**22.** appointment book
табличка с именем	**9.** nameplate	персональный календарь	**23.** organizer/ personal planner
подстилка	**10.** desk pad	хронокарта	**24.** timesheet
корзина для мусора	**11.** wastebasket	зарплата, выданная чеком	**25.** paycheck
кресло	**12.** posture chair/ clerical chair		

нож для писем	**26.** letter opener
ножницы	**27.** scissors
компостер	**28.** punch
компостер, делающий три дырки	**29.** 3-hole punch
штемпельная подушка	**30.** stamp/ink pad
штемпель	**31.** rubber stamp
ручка	**32.** pen
карандаш	**33.** pencil
механический карандаш	**34.** mechanical pencil
хайлайтер	**35.** highlighter (pen)
ластик/ стирательная резина	**36.** eraser

[1–15]
A. Welcome to the company.
B. Thank you.
A. How do you like your _____?
B. It's/They're very nice.

[16–36]
A. My desk is such a mess! I can't find my _____!
B. Here it is/Here they are next to your _____.

Which items on this page do you have? Do you have an appointment book, personal planner, or calendar? How do you remember important things such as appointments, meetings, and birthdays?

КАНЦЕЛЯРСКИЕ ТОВАРЫ

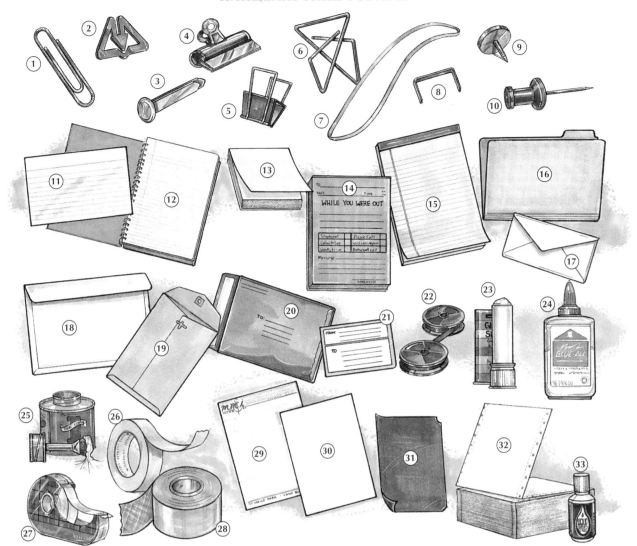

канцелярская скрепка	**1.** paper clip	блокнот с клейкими листами	**13.** Post-It note pad	резиновый клей	**25.** rubber cement
пластмассовая скрепка	**2.** plastic clip	блокнот для телефонных звонков	**14.** message pad	клейкая лента	**26.** masking tape
скрепка	**3.** paper fastener	тетрадь	**15.** legal pad	скотч лента	**27.** Scotch tape/ cellophane tape
скрепка с зажимом	**4.** bulldog clip	бумажная папка	**16.** file folder/ manila folder	лента для посылок	**28.** sealing tape/ package mailing tape
скрепка-зажим	**5.** binder clip				
зажим	**6.** clamp	конверт	**17.** envelope	писчая бумага	**29.** stationery
резинка	**7.** rubber band	каталожный конверт	**18.** catalog envelope	бумага для	**30.** typing paper
скрепка	**8.** staple	конверт с заклёпкой	**19.** clasp envelope	пишущей машины	
кнопка	**9.** thumbtack	конверт с подкладкой	**20.** mailer	копировальная бумага	**31.** carbon paper
кнопка	**10.** pushpin	почтовая наклейка	**21.** mailing label	компьютерная бумага	**32.** computer paper
индексная карточка	**11.** index card	лента для машинки	**22.** typewriter ribbon	жидкость для	**33.** correction fluid
блокнот	**12.** memo pad/ note pad	клей	**23.** gluestick	исправления ошибок	
		клей	**24.** glue		

A. {We've run out of __[1–23]__ s.
{We've run out of __[24–33]__.

B. I'll get some more from the supply room.

A. Could I borrow a/an/some __[1–33]__?

B. Sure. Here you are.

ФАБРИКА/ЗАВОД

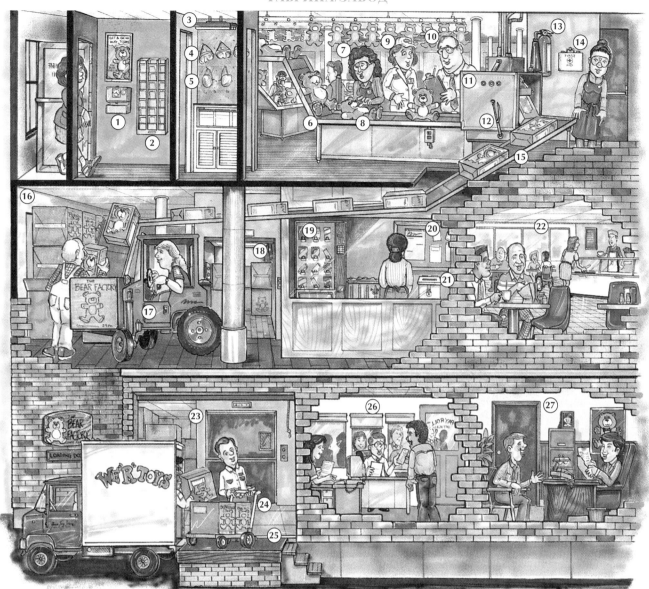

часы	**1.** time clock	мастер	**10.** foreman	автомат	**19.** vending machine
хронокарты	**2.** time cards	машина	**11.** machine	профсоюзное объявление	**20.** union notice
комната для хранения	**3.** supply room	рычаг	**12.** lever	ящик для предложений	**21.** suggestion box
защитные очки	**4.** safety glasses	огнетушитель	**13.** fire extinguisher	кафетерий/столовая	**22.** cafeteria
маски	**5.** masks	аптечка	**14.** first-aid kit	транспортный отдел	**23.** shipping department
конвейер	**6.** (assembly) line	скорой помощи			
рабочий	**7.** worker	конвейер	**15.** conveyor belt	тележка	**24.** hand truck
рабочее место	**8.** work station	склад	**16.** warehouse	погрузочный док	**25.** loading dock
ответственный за	**9.** quality control	погрузчик	**17.** forklift	касса	**26.** payroll office
качество продукции	supervisor	грузовой лифт	**18.** freight elevator	отдел кадров	**27.** personnel office

A. Excuse me. I'm a new employee. Where's/Where are the _____?
B. Next to/Near/In/On the _____.

A. Have you seen *Fred*?
B. Yes. He's in/on/at/next to/near the _____.

Are there any factories where you live? What kind? What are the working conditions there?

What products do factories in your country produce?

СТРОИТЕЛЬНЫЙ УЧАСТОК

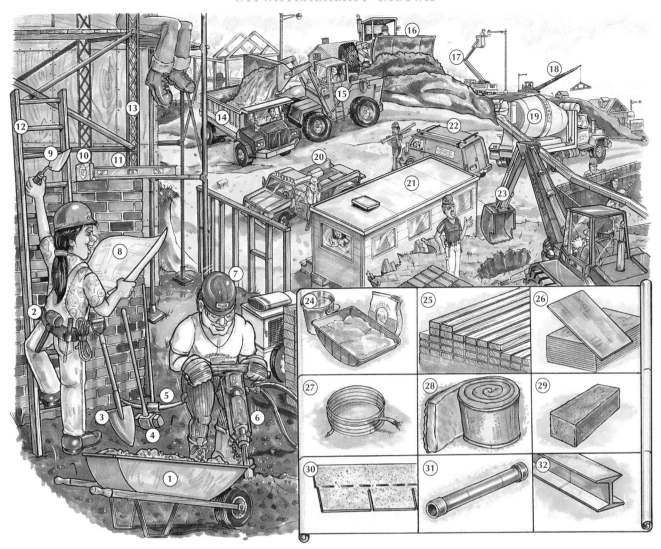

тачка	**1.** wheelbarrow	ватерпас	**11.** level	фургон	**22.** van
пояс для	**2.** toolbelt	лестница	**12.** ladder	ковш	**23.** backhoe
инструментов		строительные леса	**13.** scaffolding	цемент	**24.** cement
лопата	**3.** shovel	самосвал	**14.** dump truck	пиломатериалы	**25.** wood/lumber
кувалда	**4.** sledgehammer	грузовик	**15.** front-end loader	фанера	**26.** plywood
кирка	**5.** pickax	бульдозер	**16.** bulldozer	проволока	**27.** wire
пневматическая	**6.** jackhammer/	стрела	**17.** cherry picker	теплоизоляция	**28.** insulation
дрель	pneumatic drill	кран	**18.** crane	кирпич	**29.** brick
шлем	**7.** helmet/hard hat	цементомешалка	**19.** cement mixer	кровельная дранка	**30.** shingle
светокопия/синька	**8.** blueprints	грузовик-пикап	**20.** pickup truck	труба	**31.** pipe
мастерок	**9.** trowel	дом на колёсах	**21.** trailer	балка/перекладина	**32.** girder/beam
рулетка/сантиметр	**10.** tape measure				

[1–12]

A. Could you get me
   that/those _____?

B. Sure.

[13–23]

A. Watch out for that _____!

B. Oh! Thanks for the warning!

[24–32]

A. Are we going to have enough
   _[24–28]_ / _[29–32]_ s to finish
   the job?

B. I think so.

АВТОМОБИЛЬ

фара	1. headlight	багажник	16. trunk	воздушный фильтр	32. air filter
бампер/буфер	2. bumper	задняя фара	17. taillight	аккумулятор	33. battery
сигнал поворота	3. turn signal	тормозные огни	18. brake light	уровнемер	34. dipstick
подфонарник	4. parking light	дополнительный	19. backup light	генератор	35. alternator
шина	5. tire	сигнал		радиатор	36. radiator
колпак	6. hubcap	номерной знак	20. license plate	вентиляторный ремень	37. fan belt
капот	7. hood	выхлопная труба	21. tailpipe	шланг радиатора	38. radiator hose
лобовое стекло	8. windshield	глушитель	22. muffler	бензоколонка	39. gas station/
дворники	9. windshield wipers	коробка передач	23. transmission		service station
зеркало бокового	10. side mirror	бензобак	24. gas tank	насос	40. air pump
вида		домкрат	25. jack	станция	41. service bay
антенна	11. antenna	запасное колесо	26. spare tire	техобслуживания	
люк в крыше	12. sunroof	сигнал-вспышка	27. flare	механик	42. mechanic
автомобиля		шнур для подзарядки	28. jumper cables	работник	43. attendant
багажник	13. luggage rack/	двигатель/мотор	29. engine	бензоколонка	44. gas pump
	luggage carrier	свечи зажигания	30. spark plugs	сопло	45. nozzle
заднее стекло	14. rear windshield	карбюратор	31. carburetor		
задний дефростер	15. rear defroster				

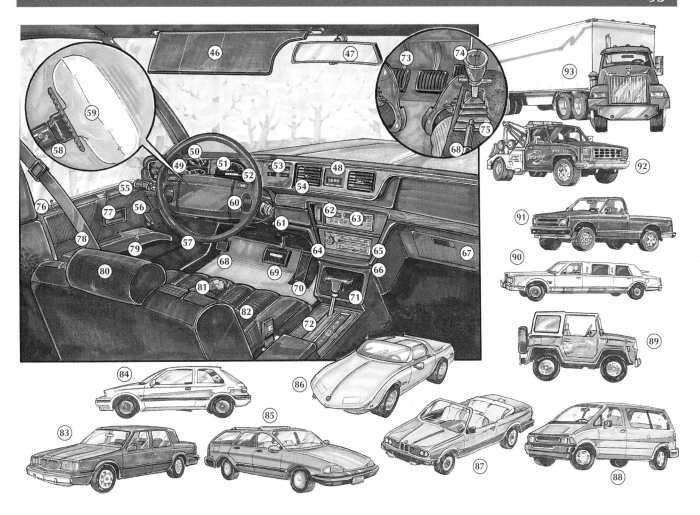

противосолнечный щиток	**46.** visor	радио	**62.** radio	дверной замок	**76.** door lock
зеркало заднего вида	**47.** rearview mirror	магнитофон	**63.** tape deck/ cassette player	дверная ручка	**77.** door handle
панель	**48.** dashboard/ instrument panel	кондиционер воздуха	**64.** air conditioning	ремень безопасности	**78.** shoulder harness
бензоуказатель	**49.** gas /fuel gauge	печка	**65.** heater	подлокотник	**79.** armrest
термометр	**50.** temperature gauge	дефростер	**66.** defroster	подголовник	**80.** headrest
спидометр	**51.** speedometer	ящик	**67.** glove compartment	ремень	**81.** seat belt
одометр	**52.** odometer	аварийный тормоз	**68.** emergency brake	сиденье	**82.** seat
предупредительные сигналы	**53.** warning lights	тормоз	**69.** brake	легковой автомобиль	**83.** sedan
вентилятор	**54.** vent	акселератор	**70.** accelerator/ gas pedal	пикап	**84.** hatchback
сигнал поворота	**55.** turn signal	переключатель скоростей	**71.** gearshift	большой пикап	**85.** station wagon
переключатель скоростей	**56.** cruise control	автоматическая трансмиссия	**72.** automatic transmission	спортивная машина	**86.** sports car
руль	**57.** steering wheel	сцепление	**73.** clutch	автомобиль с откидным верхом	**87.** convertible
рулевая колонка	**58.** steering column	переключатель	**74.** stickshift	микроавтобус	**88.** minivan
воздушный пакет	**59.** air bag	ручная трансмиссия	**75.** manual transmission	джип	**89.** jeep
гудок	**60.** horn			лимузин	**90.** limousine
зажигание	**61.** ignition			грузовик-пикап	**91.** pick-up truck
				тягач	**92.** tow truck
				грузовик с прицепом	**93.** truck

[1, 3, 8–15, 23, 34–38, 46–82]
A. What's the matter with your car?
B. The _____(s) is/are broken.

[1, 4–6, 9–11, 30–33, 37, 38]
A. Can I help you?
B. Yes. I need to replace a/the _____(s).

[1, 2, 4–8, 10–14, 16–20]
A. I was just in a car accident!
B. Oh, no! Were you hurt?
A. No. But my _____(s) was/were damaged.

туннель	**1.** tunnel	левый ряд	**14.** left lane	улица	**26.** street
мост	**2.** bridge	средний ряд	**15.** middle lane/	односторонняя улица	**27.** one-way street
будка сбора платы	**3.** tollbooth		center lane	двойная жёлтая линия	**28.** double yellow line
за проезд		правый ряд	**16.** right lane	переход	**29.** crosswalk
очередь "Без сдачи"	**4.** exact change lane	обочина	**17.** shoulder	перекрёсток	**30.** intersection
маршрутный	**5.** route sign	пунктирная линия	**18.** broken line	переход	**31.** school crossing
указатель		сплошная линия	**19.** solid line	для школьников	
скоростная дорога	**6.** highway	знак ограничения	**20.** speed limit sign	угол	**32.** corner
дорога	**7.** road	скорости		светофор	**33.** traffic light/
барьер	**8.** divider/barrier	выезд со скоростной	**21.** exit (ramp)		traffic signal
эстакада	**9.** overpass	дороги		нет левого поворота	**34.** no left turn sign
под эстакадой	**10.** underpass	съезд (знак)	**22.** exit sign	нет левого поворота	**35.** no right turn sign
въезд на скоростную	**11.** entrance ramp/	уступи дорогу (знак)	**23.** yield sign	нет разворота	**36.** no U-turn sign
дорогу	on ramp	место отдыха и услуг	**24.** service area	нет входа	**37.** do not enter sign
межштатная дорога	**12.** interstate (highway)	железнодорожный	**25.** railroad crossing	стоп	**38.** stop sign
барьер	**13.** median	переход			

A. Where's the accident?

B. It's on/in/at/near the _____.

Describe a highway you travel on.
Describe an intersection near where you live.

In your area, on which highways and streets do most accidents occur? Why are these places dangerous?

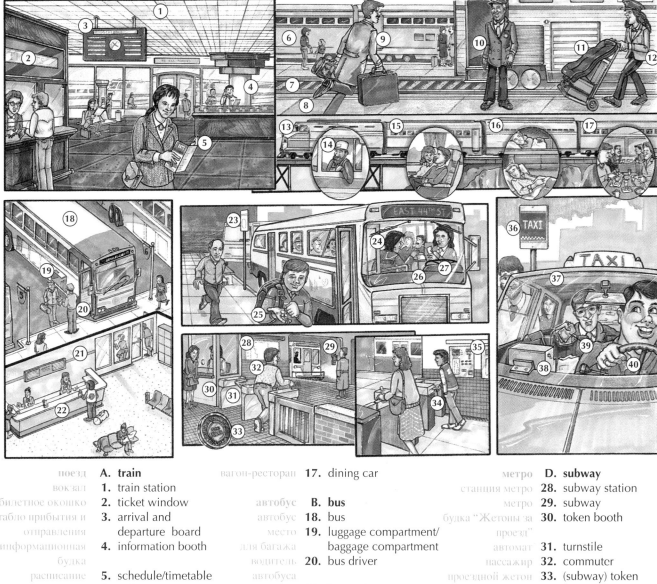

поезд	**A. train**	вагон-ресторан	**17.** dining car	метро	**D. subway**
вокзал	**1.** train station			станция метро	**28.** subway station
билетное окошко	**2.** ticket window	автобус	**B. bus**	метро	**29.** subway
табло прибытия и	**3.** arrival and	автобус	**18.** bus	будка "Жетоны за	**30.** token booth
отправления	departure board	место	**19.** luggage compartment/	проезд"	
информационная	**4.** information booth	для багажа	baggage compartment	автомат	**31.** turnstile
будка		водитель	**20.** bus driver	пассажир	**32.** commuter
расписание	**5.** schedule/timetable	автобуса		проездной жетон	**33.** (subway) token
поезд	**6.** train	автовокзал	**21.** bus station	проездной билет	**34.** fare card
рельсы	**7.** track	билетная касса	**22.** ticket counter	автомат по продаже	**35.** fare card machine
платформа	**8.** platform			проездных билетов	
пассажир	**9.** passenger	местный автобус	**C. local bus**		
кондуктор	**10.** conductor	автобусная	**23.** bus stop	такси	**E. taxi**
багаж	**11.** luggage/baggage	остановка		стоянка такси	**36.** taxi stand
носильщик	**12.** porter/redcap	пассажир	**24.** rider/passenger	такси	**37.** taxi/cab/taxicab
двигатель/мотор	**13.** engine	стоимость проезда	**25.** (bus) fare	счётчик	**38.** meter
машинист	**14.** engineer	касса для оплаты	**26.** fare box	плата	**39.** fare
пассажирский вагон	**15.** passenger car	билет для пересадки	**27.** transfer	таксист	**40.** cab driver/
спальный вагон	**16.** sleeper				taxi driver

[A–E]
A. How are you going to get there?
B. { I'm going to take the _[A–D]_ .
    { I'm going to take a _[E]_ .

[1–8, 10–23, 26, 28–31, 35, 36]
A. Excuse me. Where's the _____?
B. Over there.

АЭРОПОРТ

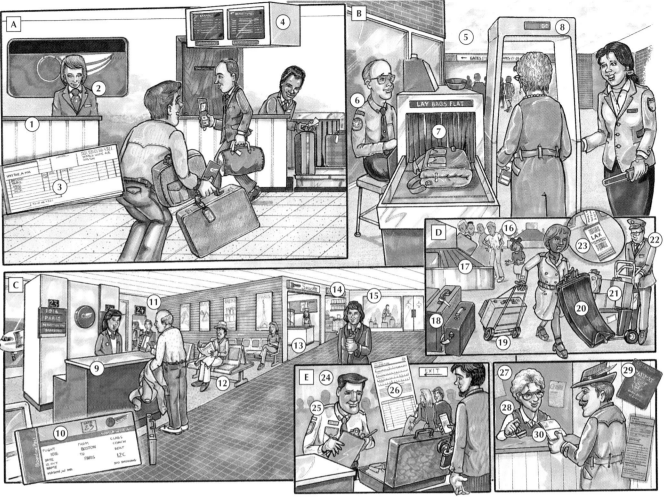

Регистрация	**A. Check-In**
билетная касса	**1.** ticket counter
агент по продаже билетов	**2.** ticket agent
билет	**3.** ticket
монитор прилёта и вылета	**4.** arrival and departure monitor
Служба безопасности	**B. Security**
пропускной пункт	**5.** security checkpoint
работник службы безопасности	**6.** security guard
установка для просмотра багажа	**7.** X-ray machine
детектор на металл	**8.** metal detector
Ворота	**C. The Gate**
стол регистрации	**9.** check-in counter
посадочный билет	**10.** boarding pass
ворота	**11.** gate
зал ожидания	**12.** waiting area
кафетерий	**13.** concession stand/snack bar
сувенирный магазин	**14.** gift shop
беспошлинный магазин	**15.** duty-free shop

Зал получения багажа	**D. Baggage Claim**
зал получения багажа	**16.** baggage claim (area)
багажная карусель	**17.** baggage carousel
чемодан	**18.** suitcase
багажная тележка	**19.** luggage carrier
чемодан для одежды	**20.** garment bag
багаж	**21.** baggage
носильщик	**22.** porter/skycap
багажный номерок	**23.** (baggage) claim check
Таможня и иммиграционная служба	**E. Customs and Immigration**
таможня	**24.** customs
таможенник	**25.** customs officer
таможенная декларация	**26.** customs declaration form
иммиграционная служба	**27.** immigration
работник иммиграционной службы	**28.** immigration officer
паспорт	**29.** passport
виза	**30.** visa

[1, 2, 4–9, 11–17, 24, 25, 27, 28]
A. Excuse me. Where's the _____?*
B. Right over there.

*With 24 and 27, use: Excuse me. Where's _____?

[3, 10, 18–21, 23, 26, 29, 30]
A. Oh, no! I think I've lost my _____!
B. I'll help you look for it.

кабина	1. cockpit	сиденье в проходе	18. aisle seat	аэровокзал	33. terminal (building)
пилот	2. pilot/captain	Пристегните ремни	19. Fasten Seat Belt sign	контрольно-диспетчерский пункт	34. control tower
второй пилот	3. co-pilot	Не курить	20. No Smoking sign	самолёт	35. airplane/plane/jet
пульт управления	4. instrument panel	кнопка для вызова	21. call button	нос	36. nose
бортинженер	5. flight engineer	кислородная маска	22. oxygen mask	фюзеляж	37. fuselage
места первого класса	6. first-class section	аварийный выход	23. emergency exit	грузовая дверь	38. cargo door
пассажир	7. passenger	подлокотник	24. armrest	шасси	39. landing gear
пищеблок	8. galley	кнопка управления сиденьем	25. seat control	крыло	40. wing
стюардесса	9. flight attendant			двигатель/мотор	41. engine
туалет	10. lavatory/bathroom	столик	26. tray (table)	хвост	42. tail
салон	11. cabin	еда	27. meal	винтомоторный	43. propeller plane/prop
ручная кладь	12. carry-on bag	карман	28. seat pocket	самолёт	
верхний ящик	13. overhead compartment	карта-инструкция при аварии	29. emergency instruction card	пропеллер	44. propeller
проход	14. aisle	пакет	30. air sickness bag	вертолёт	45. helicopter
ремень	15. seat belt	спасательный жилет	31. life vest	несущий винт	46. rotor (blade)
сиденье у окна	16. window seat	взлётно-посадочная полоса	32. runway		
сиденье посередине	17. middle seat				

A. Where's the _____?

B. In/On/Next to/Behind/In front of/Above/Below the _____.

Ladies and gentlemen. This is your captain speaking. I'm sorry for the delay. We had a little problem with one of our _____s.* Everything is fine now and we'll be taking off shortly.

*Use 4, 7, 10, 12, 20–22, 24.

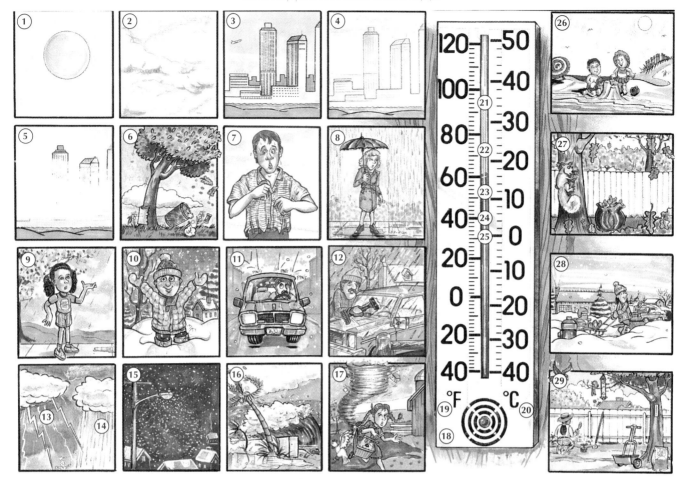

Погода	A. Weather					
солнечный	1. sunny	дождь со снегом	12. sleeting	жаркий	21. hot
облачный	2. cloudy	молния	13. lightning	тёплый	22. warm
ясный	3. clear	гроза	14. thunderstorm	прохладный	23. cool
туманный	4. hazy	вьюга/метель/	15. snowstorm	холодный	24. cold
туманный	5. foggy	снежный буран		очень холодно	25. freezing
ветреный	6. windy	ураган	16. hurricane/typhoon		
влажный	7. humid/muggy	торнадо	17. tornado	Времена года	C. Seasons
идёт дождь	8. raining			лето	26. summer
моросит	9. drizzling	Температура	B. Temperature	осень	27. fall/autumn
идёт снег	10. snowing	термометр	18. thermometer	зима	28. winter
идёт град	11. hailing	шкала Фаренгейта	19. Fahrenheit	весна	29. spring
		шкала Цельсия	20. Centigrade/Celsius		

[1–12]
A. What's the weather like?
B. It's _____.

[13–17]
A. What's the weather forecast?
B. There's going to be
   [13] /a [14–17] .

[19–25]
A. How's the weather?
B. It's [21–25] .
A. What's the temperature?
B. It's .... degrees [19, 20] .

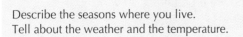

Describe the seasons where you live.
Tell about the weather and the temperature.

What's your favorite season?
Why?

Кемпинг	**A. Camping**		Поход	**B. Hiking**		Подъём по скале	**D. Rock Climbing**
палатка	**1.** tent		походные ботинки	**8.** hiking boots		верёвка	**12.** rope
рюкзак	**2.** backpack		компас	**9.** compass		страховочный пояс	**13.** harness
спальный мешок	**3.** sleeping bag		карта троп	**10.** trail map			
колья	**4.** tent stakes					Пикник	**E. Picnic**
топорик	**5.** hatchet		Восхождение/подъёма	**C. Mountain Climbing**		одеяло	**14.** (picnic) blanket
фонарь	**6.** lantern		на гору			термос	**15.** thermos
походная плита	**7.** camp stove		походные ботинки	**11.** hiking boots		корзинка для пикника	**16.** picnic basket

[A–E]
A. Let's go _____* this weekend.
B. Good idea! We haven't gone _____*
   in a long time.

*With E, say: on a picnic

[1–16]
A. Did you bring the _____?
B. Yes, I did.

Have you ever gone camping or hiking?
Where? What equipment did you use?

Do you like to go on picnics? Where?
What picnic supplies and food do you take with you?

беговая дорожка	**1.** jogging path	зоопарк	**10.** zoo	игровая площадка	**18.** playground
туалеты	**2.** rest rooms	фонтанчик для питья	**11.** water fountain	"Джунгли"	**19.** jungle gym
статуя/памятник	**3.** statue	эстрада-ракушка	**12.** band shell	брусья	**20.** monkey bars
место для пикника	**4.** picnic area	верховая тропа	**13.** bridle path	горка	**21.** slide
стол для пикника	**5.** picnic table	подставка	**14.** bike rack	качели	**22.** swings
рашпер	**6.** grill	для велосипедов		качели	**23.** tire swing
ящик для мусора	**7.** trash can	утиный пруд	**15.** duck pond	доска-качели	**24.** seesaw
карусель	**8.** merry-go-round/	велосипедная	**16.** bicycle path/	мелкий бассейн	**25.** wading pool
	carousel	дорожка	bikeway	песочница	**26.** sandbox
фонтан	**9.** fountain	скамья	**17.** bench	песок	**27.** sand

[1–18] A. Excuse me. Does this park have (a) _____?
B. Yes. Right over there.

[19–27] A. { Be careful on the [19–24] !
{ Be careful in the [25–27] !
B. I will, Mom/Dad.

Describe a park and a playground you are familiar with.

ПЛЯЖ

спасатель	**1.** lifeguard	замок из песка	**12.** sand castle	надувной матрац	**22.** raft/air mattress
спасательная будка	**2.** lifeguard stand	ракушка	**13.** seashell/shell	камера	**23.** tube
спасательный круг	**3.** life preserver	пляжный зонт	**14.** beach umbrella	одеяло	**24.** (beach) blanket
закусочный бар	**4.** snack bar/ refreshment stand	пляжный стул	**15.** (beach) chair	шапка от солнца	**25.** sun hat
		пляжное полотенце	**16.** (beach) towel	солнечные очки	**26.** sunglasses
песчаная дюна	**5.** sand dune	купальный костюм	**17.** bathing suit/ swimsuit	крем для загара	**27.** suntan lotion/ sunscreen
камень	**6.** rock				
пловец	**7.** swimmer	купальная шапочка	**18.** bathing cap	ведро	**28.** pail/bucket
волна	**8.** wave	доска для катания по	**19.** kickboard	лопата	**29.** shovel
сёрфер	**9.** surfer	волнам		пляжный мяч	**30.** beach ball
продавец	**10.** vendor	доска для сёрфинга	**20.** surfboard	охладитель	**31.** cooler
загорающий	**11.** sunbather	бумажный змей	**21.** kite		

[1–13]
A. What a nice beach!
B. It is. Look at all the _____s!

[14–31]
A. Are you ready for the beach?
B. Almost. I just have to get my _____.

Do you like to go to the beach? Describe your favorite beach. What do you take when you go there?

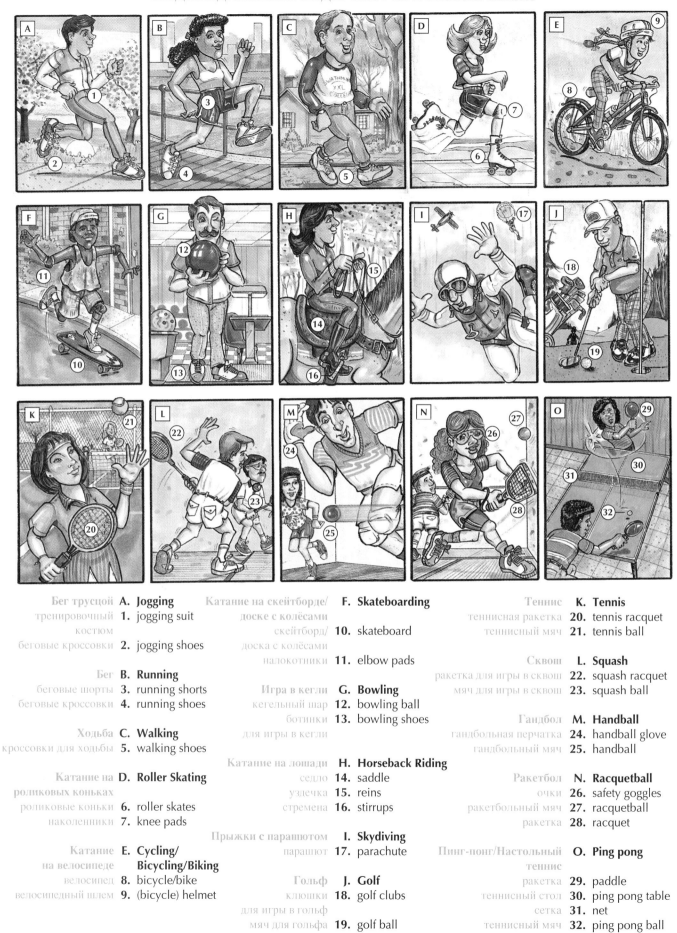

| Бег трусцой **A. Jogging** | | Катание на скейтборде/ | **F. Skateboarding** | Теннис | **K. Tennis** |

Бег трусцой **A. Jogging**
тренировочный **1.** jogging suit
костюм
беговые кроссовки **2.** jogging shoes

Бег **B. Running**
беговые шорты **3.** running shorts
беговые кроссовки **4.** running shoes

Ходьба **C. Walking**
кроссовки для ходьбы **5.** walking shoes

Катание на **D. Roller Skating**
роликовых коньках
роликовые коньки **6.** roller skates
наколенники **7.** knee pads

Катание **E. Cycling/**
на велосипеде **Bicycling/Biking**
велосипед **8.** bicycle/bike
велосипедный шлем **9.** (bicycle) helmet

Катание на скейтборде/
доске с колёсами
скейтборд **10.** skateboard
доска с колёсами
налокотники **11.** elbow pads

Игра в кегли **G. Bowling**
кегельный шар **12.** bowling ball
ботинки **13.** bowling shoes
для игры в кегли

Катание на лошади **H. Horseback Riding**
седло **14.** saddle
уздечка **15.** reins
стремена **16.** stirrups

Прыжки с парашютом **I. Skydiving**
парашют **17.** parachute

Гольф **J. Golf**
клюшки **18.** golf clubs
для игры в гольф
мяч для гольфа **19.** golf ball

F. Skateboarding

Теннис **K. Tennis**
теннисная ракетка **20.** tennis racquet
теннисный мяч **21.** tennis ball

Сквош **L. Squash**
ракетка для игры в сквош **22.** squash racquet
мяч для игры в сквош **23.** squash ball

Гандбол **M. Handball**
гандбольная перчатка **24.** handball glove
гандбольный мяч **25.** handball

Ракетбол **N. Racquetball**
очки **26.** safety goggles
ракетбольный мяч **27.** racquetball
ракетка **28.** racquet

Пинг-понг/Настольный **O. Ping pong**
теннис
ракетка **29.** paddle
теннисный стол **30.** ping pong table
сетка **31.** net
теннисный мяч **32.** ping pong ball

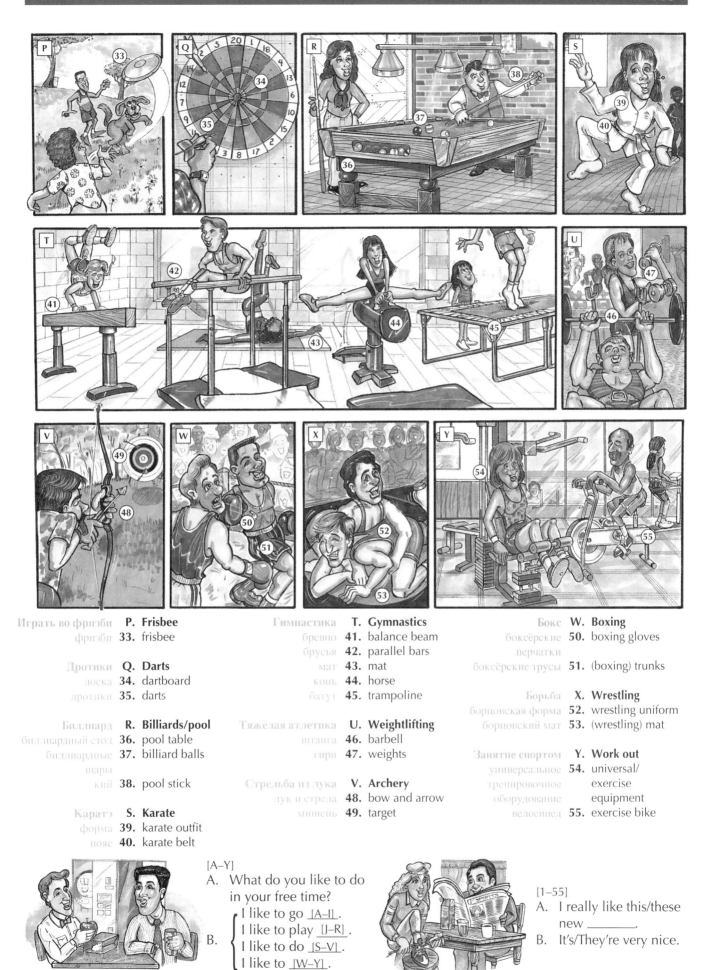

Играть во фризби	**P. Frisbee**	Гимнастика	**T. Gymnastics**	Бокс	**W. Boxing**
фризби	**33.** frisbee	бревно	**41.** balance beam	боксёрские	**50.** boxing gloves
		брусья	**42.** parallel bars	перчатки	
Дротики	**Q. Darts**	мат	**43.** mat	боксёрские трусы	**51.** (boxing) trunks
доска	**34.** dartboard	конь	**44.** horse		
дротики	**35.** darts	батут	**45.** trampoline	Борьба	**X. Wrestling**
				борцовская форма	**52.** wrestling uniform
Биллиард	**R. Billiards/pool**	Тяжёлая атлетика	**U. Weightlifting**	борцовский мат	**53.** (wrestling) mat
биллиардный стол	**36.** pool table	штанга	**46.** barbell		
биллиардные	**37.** billiard balls	гири	**47.** weights	Занятие спортом	**Y. Work out**
шары				универсальное	**54.** universal/
кий	**38.** pool stick	Стрельба из лука	**V. Archery**	тренировочное	exercise
		лук и стрела	**48.** bow and arrow	оборудование	equipment
Каратэ	**S. Karate**	мишень	**49.** target	велосипед	**55.** exercise bike
форма	**39.** karate outfit				
пояс	**40.** karate belt				

[A–Y]
A. What do you like to do in your free time?
B. { I like to go [A–I].
I like to play [J–R].
I like to do [S–V].
I like to [W–Y].

[1–55]
A. I really like this/these new _____.
B. It's/They're very nice.

КОМАНДНЫЕ ВИДЫ СПОРТА

[A–H]
A. Do you like **baseball**?
B. Yes. **Baseball** is one of my favorite sports.

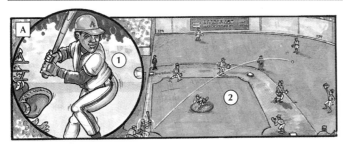

Бейсбол **A. Baseball**	Лакросс **D. Lacrosse**	Волейбол **G. Volleyball**
бейсболист **1.** baseball player	лакроссист **7.** lacrosse player	волейболист **13.** volleyball player
бейсбольное поле **2.** baseball field/ ballfield	лакроссное поле **8.** lacrosse field	волейбольная площадка **14.** volleyball court
	Хоккей E. (Ice) Hockey	
Софтбол **B. Softball**	хоккеист **9.** hockey player	Футбол **H. Soccer**
софтболист **3.** softball player	хоккейная **10.** hockey rink	футболист **15.** soccer player
поле для игры в софтбол **4.** ballfield	площадка	футбольное поле **16.** soccer field
Американский футбол **C. Football**	Баскетбол **F. Basketball**	
футболист **5.** football player	баскетболист **11.** basketball player	
футбольное поле **6.** football field	баскетбольная **12.** basketball court	
	площадка	

A. .... plays [A–H] very well.
B. You're right. I think he's/she's one of the best _____s* on the team.

*Use 1, 3, 5, 7, 9, 11, 13, 15.

A. Now, listen! I want all of you to go out on that _____† and play the best game of [A–H] you've ever played!
B. All right, Coach!

†Use 2, 4, 6, 8, 10, 12, 14, 16.

Which sports on this page do you like to play? Which do you like to watch?
What are your favorite teams?
Name some famous players of these sports.

[1–27]
A. I can't find my **baseball**!
B. Look in the *closet*.*

*closet, basement, garage

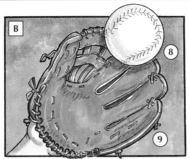

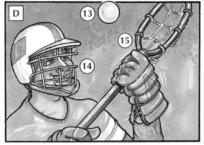

Бейсбол	**A. Baseball**	Американский футбол	**C. Football**	Баскетбол	**F. Basketball**
бейсбольный мяч	**1.** baseball	футбольный мяч	**10.** football	баскетбольный мяч	**21.** basketball
лапта/бита	**2.** bat	футбольный шлем	**11.** football helmet	баскетбольный щит	**22.** backboard
шлем	**3.** batting helmet	наплечники	**12.** shoulder pads	баскетбольная	**23.** basketball hoop
бейсбольная форма	**4.** baseball uniform			корзина	
маска	**5.** catcher's mask	Лакросс	**D. Lacrosse**		
бейсбольные	**6.** baseball glove	лакроссный мяч	**13.** lacrosse ball	Волейбол	**G. Volleyball**
перчатки	**7.** catcher's mitt	маска	**14.** face guard	волейбольный мяч	**24.** volleyball
ловушка		лакроссная клюшка	**15.** lacrosse stick	волейбольная сетка	**25.** volleyball net
		Хоккей	**E. Hockey**		
Софтбол	**B. Softball**	хоккейная шайба	**16.** hockey puck	Футбол	**H. Soccer**
софтбольный мяч	**8.** softball	хоккейная клюшка	**17.** hockey stick	футбольный мяч	**26.** soccer ball
софтбольная	**9.** softball glove	хоккейная маска	**18.** hockey mask	щитки	**27.** shinguards
перчатка		хоккейные перчатки	**19.** hockey glove		
		хоккейные коньки	**20.** hockey skates		

[In a store]
A. Excuse me. I'm looking for
    (a) [1–27] .
B. All our [A–H] equipment is over
    there.
A. Thanks.

[At home]
A. I'm going to play [A–H] after
    school today.
B. Don't forget your [1–21, 24–27] !

Which sports on this page are popular
in your country? Which sports are
played in high school?

ЗИМНИЕ ВИДЫ СПОРТА И ОТДЫХА

[A–H]
A. What's your favorite winter sport?
B. **Skiing**.

Горнолыжный **A. (Downhill) Skiing**
спорт
лыжи **1.** skis
лыжные ботинки **2.** ski boots
крепление **3.** bindings
палки **4.** poles

Катание на **B. Cross-country**
лыжах **Skiing**
лыжи **5.** cross-country skis

Катание на коньках **C. (Ice) Skating**
коньки **6.** (ice) skates
чехлы для коньков **7.** skate guards

Фигурное катание **D. Figure Skating**
фигурные коньки **8.** figure skates

Катание на санках/салазка **E. Sledding**
санки/салазки **9.** sled
тарелка **10.** sledding dish/
для катания с гор   saucer

Катание на бобслее **F. Bobsledding**
бобслей **11.** bobsled

Катание на аэросанях **G. Snowmobiling**
аэросани **12.** snowmobile

Катание на санях **H. Tobogganing**
сани **13.** toboggan

[A–H]
[At work or at school on Friday]
A. What are you going to do this
   weekend?
B. I'm going to go _____.

[1–13]
[On the telephone]
A. Hello. Jimmy's Sporting Goods.
B. Hello. Do you sell _____(s)?
A. Yes, we do./No, we don't.

Have you ever watched the Winter
Olympics? What is your favorite
event? Which event do you think
is the most exciting? the most
dangerous?

ВОДНЫЕ ВИДЫ СПОРТА И ОТДЫХА

[A–L]
A. Would you like to go **sailing** tomorrow?
B. Sure. I'd love to.

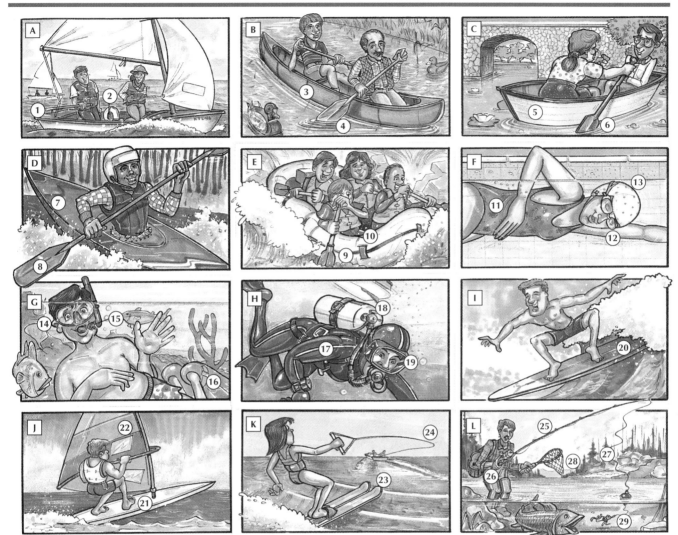

Парусный спорт	**A. Sailing**	Плавание	**F. Swimming**	Виндсёрфинг	**J. Windsurfing**
парусная лодка	**1.** sailboat	купальный костюм	**11.** swimsuit/ bathing suit	доска для виндсёрфинга	**21.** sailboard
спасательный жилет	**2.** life preserver	очки	**12.** goggles	парус	**22.** sail
Катание на каноэ	**B. Canoeing**	купальная шапочка	**13.** bathing cap	Катание	**K. Waterskiing**
каноэ	**3.** canoe	Плавание под водой с	**G. Snorkeling**	на водных лыжах	
вёсла	**4.** paddles	маской и трубкой		водные лыжи	**23.** water skis
Катание на лодке	**C. Rowing**	маска	**14.** mask	буксирный канат	**24.** towrope
гребная лодка	**5.** rowboat	трубка	**15.** snorkel		
вёсла	**6.** oars	ласты	**16.** flippers	Рыбная ловля	**L. Fishing**
Катание на байдарке	**D. Kayaking**	Плавание под водой	**H. Scuba Diving**	удочка	**25.** (fishing) rod
байдарка	**7.** kayak	с аквалангом		катушка	**26.** reel
весло	**8.** paddle	костюм	**17.** wet suit	лёска	**27.** (fishing) line
Катание на плоту	**E. (White Water) Rafting**	акваланг	**18.** (air) tank	сеть	**28.** net
		маска для ныряния	**19.** (diving) mask	приманка	**29.** bait
плот	**9.** raft	Сёрфинг	**I. Surfing**		
спасательный жилет	**10.** life jacket	доска для сёрфинга	**20.** surfboard		

СПОРТИВНЫЕ ДВИЖЕНИЯ И ДВИЖЕНИЯ ПРИ ВЫПОЛНЕНИИ УПРАЖНЕНИЙ

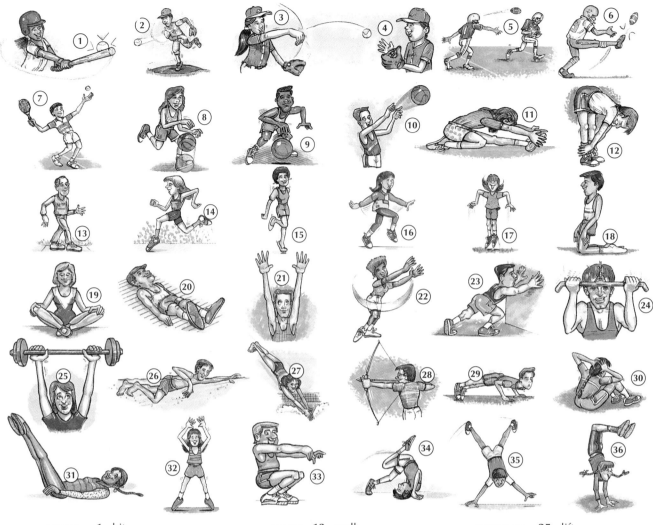

ударить	**1.** hit	ходить	**13.** walk	поднимать	**25.** lift
бросать	**2.** pitch	бегать	**14.** run	плавать	**26.** swim
бросать	**3.** throw	скакать/прыгать	**15.** hop	нырять	**27.** dive
ловить	**4.** catch	скакать	**16.** skip	стрелять	**28.** shoot
передавать	**5.** pass	прыгать	**17.** jump	отжимание от пола	**29.** push-up
ударить	**6.** kick	встать на колени	**18.** kneel	приседание	**30.** sit-up
подавать	**7.** serve	сидеть	**19.** sit	поднимание ног	**31.** leg lift
бить мяч об пол	**8.** bounce	лежать	**20.** lie down	прыжки с руками	**32.** jumping jack
вести	**9.** dribble	достать руками	**21.** reach	глубокое приседание	**33.** deep knee bend
бросать	**10.** shoot	размахивать	**22.** swing	сальто	**34.** somersault
растягивать	**11.** stretch	отжиматься от стены	**23.** push	кувырок колесом	**35.** cartwheel
согнуться	**12.** bend	подтягиваться	**24.** pull	стойка на руках	**36.** handstand

[1–10] A. _____ the ball!
     B. Okay, Coach!

[11–28] A. Now _____!
     B. Like this?
     A. Yes.

[29–36] A. Okay, everybody. I want
     you to do twenty _____s!
     B. Twenty _____s?!
     A. That's right.

Do you exercise regularly?
Which exercises do you do?

Be an exercise instructor. Lead your friends in an exercise
routine using the actions on this page.

[A–Q]
A. What's your hobby?
B. **Sewing.**

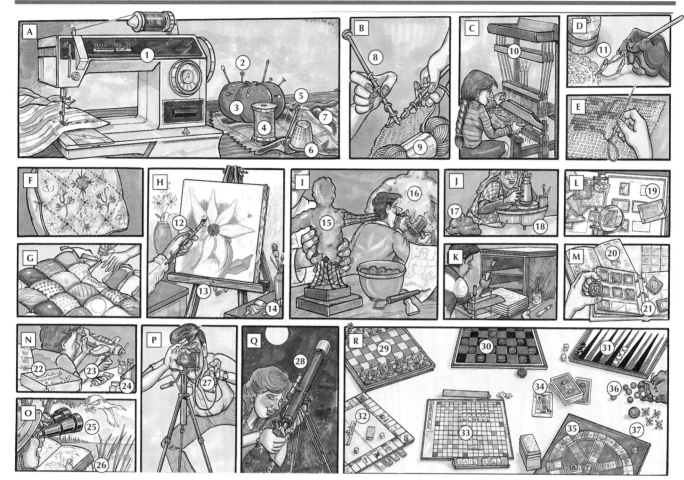

Шитьё	**A. Sewing**	мольберт	**13.** easel	краска	**24.** (model) paint

Шитьё **A. Sewing**
швейная машина **1.** sewing machine
шпилька/булавка **2.** pin
подушка для булавок **3.** pin cushion
нитки **4.** thread
швейная игла **5.** (sewing) needle
напёрсток **6.** thimble
материя **7.** material

вязание **B. Knitting**
вязальные спицы **8.** knitting needle
пряжа/нитки **9.** yarn

Тканьё **C. Weaving**
ткацкий станок **10.** loom

Вязание крючком **D. Crocheting**
вязальный крючок **11.** crochet hook

Рукоделие **E. Needlepoint**

Вышивание **F. Embroidery**

Стегание **G. Quilting**

Рисование **H. Painting**
кисть **12.** paintbrush

мольберт **13.** easel
краски **14.** paint

Лепка **I. Sculpting/sculpture**
гипс **15.** plaster
камень **16.** stone

Керамика **J. Pottery**
глина **17.** clay
гончарный круг **18.** potter's wheel

Работа по дереву **K. Woodworking**

Коллекционирование **L. Stamp Collecting**
марок
альбом для марок **19.** stamp album

Коллекционирование **M. Coin Collecting**
монет
каталог монет **20.** coin catalog
альбом монет **21.** coin album

Моделирование **N. Model Building**
набор для **22.** model kit
моделирования
клей **23.** (model) glue

краска **24.** (model) paint

Наблюдение за птицами **O. Bird Watching**
бинокль **25.** binoculars
справочник **26.** field guide

Фотографирование **P. Photography**
фотоаппарат **27.** camera

Астрономия **Q. Astronomy**
телескоп **28.** telescope

Игры **R. Games**
шахматы **29.** chess
шашки **30.** checkers
триктрак **31.** backgammon
"Монополия" **32.** Monopoly
Эрудит **33.** Scrabble
карты **34.** cards
"Тривиальные вопросы" **35.** Trivial Pursuit
игра в стеклянные **36.** marbles
шарики
джекс **37.** jacks

[1–28]   [In a store]
A. May I help you?
B. Yes, please. I'd like to buy (a/an) _____.

[29–37]   [At home]
A. What do you want to do?
B. Let's play _____.

What's your hobby?
What games are popular in your country? Describe how to play one.

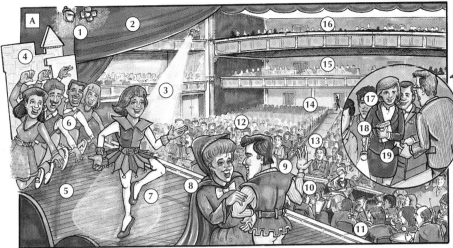

Театр	**A. Theater**			
свет	**1.** lights/lighting	амфитеатр	**15.** mezzanine	
занавес	**2.** curtain	балкон	**16.** balcony	
прожектор	**3.** spotlight	билетёр	**17.** usher	
декорации	**4.** scenery	программа	**18.** program	
сцена	**5.** stage	билет	**19.** ticket	
хор	**6.** chorus			
танцор	**7.** dancer	**Симфония**	**B. Symphony**	
актриса	**8.** actress	симфонический оркестр	**20.** symphony orchestra	
актёр	**9.** actor	музыкант	**21.** musician	
оркестр	**10.** orchestra	дирижёр	**22.** conductor	
оркестровая яма	**11.** orchestra pit	дирижёрская палочка	**23.** baton	
зрители	**12.** audience	подиум	**24.** podium	
проход	**13.** aisle			
партер	**14.** orchestra	**Опера**	**C. Opera**	
		оперный певец	**25.** opera singer	
		оперная труппа	**26.** opera company	

Балет	**D. Ballet**
балеро	**27.** ballet dance
балерина	**28.** ballerina
балетная труппа	**29.** ballet company
балетные тапочки	**30.** ballet slippers
балетные тапочки	**31.** toeshoes

Кино	**E. Movies**
афиша	**32.** marquee
билетная касса	**33.** box office
киноафиша	**34.** billboard
фойе	**35.** lobby
буфет	**36.** refreshment stand
киноэкрана	**37.** (movie) screen

[A–E]
A. What are you doing this evening?
B. I'm going to the _____.

[1–11, 20–37]
A. { What a magnificent _____!
{ What magnificent _____s!
B. I agree.

[14–16]
A. Where did you sit during the performance?
B. We sat in the _____.

What kinds of entertainment on this page are popular in your country?

Tell about a play, concert, opera, ballet, or movie you have seen. Describe the performance and the theater.

ВИДЫ РАЗВЛЕЧЕНИЯ

Музыка	**A. Music**	Пьесы	**B. Plays**	научно-фантастический	**23.** science fiction
классическая музыка	**1.** classical music	драма	**13.** drama	фильм	movie
популярная музыка	**2.** popular music	комедия	**14.** comedy		
ковбойская музыка	**3.** country music	музыкальная	**15.** musical (comedy)	Телевизионные	**D. TV Programs**
рок-музыка	**4.** rock music	комедия		программы	
народная музыка	**5.** folk music			драма	**24.** drama
рэп-музыка	**6.** rap music	Кино	**C. Movies**	ситуационная	**25.** (situation)
евангелистская музыка	**7.** gospel music	драма	**16.** drama	комедия	comedy/sitcom
джаз	**8.** jazz	комедия	**17.** comedy	ток шоу	**26.** talk show
блюз	**9.** blues	вестерн	**18.** western	игровое шоу	**27.** game show
блуграсс	**10.** bluegrass	мультфильм	**19.** cartoon	новости	**28.** news program
тяжёлый рок/хеви метал	**11.** heavy metal	зарубежный фильм	**20.** foreign film	спортивная программа	**29.** sports program
регги	**12.** reggae	приключенческий	**21.** adventure movie	детская программа	**30.** children's program
		фильм		мультфильм	**31.** cartoon
		военный фильм	**22.** war movie		

A. What kind of __[A–D]__ do you like?

B. { I like __[1–12]__ .
    { I like __[13–31]__ s.

What's your favorite type of music?
Who is your favorite singer? musician?
  musical group?

What kind of movies do you like?
Who are your favorite movie stars?
What are the titles of your favorite
  movies?

What kind of TV programs do you like?
What are your favorite shows?

МУЗЫКАЛЬНЫЕ ИНСТРУМЕНТЫ

A. Do you play a musical instrument?
B. Yes. I play the **violin**.

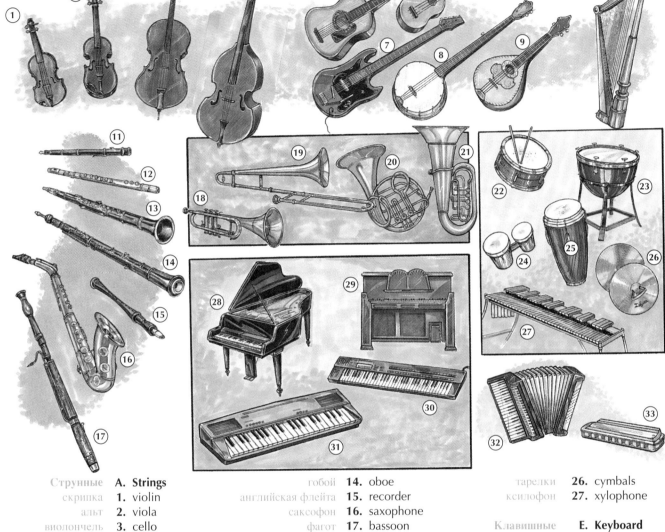

Струнные	**A. Strings**		гобой	**14.** oboe	тарелки	**26.** cymbals
скрипка	**1.** violin		английская флейта	**15.** recorder	ксилофон	**27.** xylophone
альт	**2.** viola		саксофон	**16.** saxophone		
виолончель	**3.** cello		фагот	**17.** bassoon	**Клавишные**	**E. Keyboard**
контрабас	**4.** bass				**инструменты**	**Instruments**
акустическая гитара	**5.** (acoustic) guitar		**Духовые**	**C. Brass**	рояль/пианино	**28.** piano
гавайская гитара	**6.** ukelele		труба	**18.** trumpet	орган	**29.** organ
электрогитара	**7.** electric guitar		тромбон	**19.** trombone	электропианино	**30.** electric piano/
банджо	**8.** banjo		валторна	**20.** French horn		digital piano
мандолина	**9.** mandolin		туба	**21.** tuba	синтезатор	**31.** synthesizer
арфа	**10.** harp					
			Ударные инструменты	**D. Percussion**	**Другие**	**F. Other**
Деревянные духовые	**B. Woodwinds**		барабан	**22.** drum	**инструменты**	**Instruments**
пикколо	**11.** piccolo		литавра	**23.** kettle drum	аккордеон	**32.** accordion
флейта	**12.** flute		бонджоуз	**24.** bongos	гармоника	**33.** harmonica
кларнет	**13.** clarinet		конга (барабан)	**25.** conga (drum)		

A. You play the _____ very well.
B. Thank you.

A. What's that noise?
B. That's my son/daughter practicing the _____.

Do you play a musical instrument? Which one?
Name and describe other musical instruments used in your country.

дерево	**1.** tree	клён	**18.** maple	гардения	**34.** gardenia
лист – листья	**2.** leaf–leaves	дуб	**19.** oak	лилия	**35.** lily
ветка/прут	**3.** twig	сосна	**20.** pine	анютины глазки	**36.** pansy
ветка/ветвь	**4.** branch	красное дерево	**21.** redwood	петуния	**37.** petunia
сук/ветвь	**5.** limb	плакучая ива	**22.** (weeping) willow	орхидея	**38.** orchid
ствол	**6.** trunk	цветок	**23.** flower	роза	**39.** rose
кора	**7.** bark	лепесток	**24.** petal	подсолнечник	**40.** sunflower
корень	**8.** root	пестик	**25.** pistula	тюльпан	**41.** tulip
игла	**9.** needle	тычинка	**26.** stamen	фиалка	**42.** violet
шишка	**10.** cone	стебель	**27.** stem	куст/кустарник	**43.** bush
кизил	**11.** dogwood	бутон	**28.** bud	куст	**44.** shrub
остролист	**12.** holly	шип	**29.** thorn	папоротник	**45.** fern
магнолия	**13.** magnolia	луковица	**30.** bulb	растение	**46.** plant
вяз	**14.** elm	хризантема	**31.** chrysanthemum/	кактус – кактусы	**47.** cactus–cacti
вишня	**15.** cherry		mum	лоза	**48.** vine
пальма	**16.** palm	жёлтый нарцисс	**32.** daffodil	трава	**49.** grass
берёза	**17.** birch	ромашка	**33.** daisy	сумак	**50.** poison ivy

[11–22]
A. What kind of tree is that?
B. I think it's a/an _____ tree.

[31–48]
A. Look at all the _____s!
B. They're beautiful!

Describe your favorite tree and your favorite flower.
What kinds of trees and flowers grow where you live?

In your country, are flowers used at weddings? at funerals?
on holidays? on visits to the hospital? Tell which flowers are
used for different occasions.

лес	**1.** forest/woods	скала	**13.** cliff	кислотный дождь	**25.** acid rain
озеро	**2.** lake	каньон	**14.** canyon	ядовитые отходы	**26.** toxic waste
луг	**3.** meadow	река	**15.** river	радиация	**27.** radiation
гора	**4.** mountain	плотина	**16.** dam	загрязнение воздуха	**28.** water pollution
долина	**5.** valley	пустыня	**17.** desert	нефть	**29.** oil
водопад	**6.** waterfall	дюна	**18.** dune	натуральный газ	**30.** (natural) gas
речные пороги	**7.** rapids	джунгли	**19.** jungle	уголь	**31.** coal
холм	**8.** hill	морское побережье	**20.** seashore	ветер	**32.** wind
поле	**9.** field	залив	**21.** bay	ядерная энергия	**33.** nuclear energy
ручей	**10.** stream/brook	океан	**22.** ocean	солнечная энергия	**34.** solar energy
пруд	**11.** pond	остров	**23.** island	гидроэлектроэнергия	**35.** hydroelectric power
плато	**12.** plateau	загрязнение воздуха	**24.** air pollution		

[1–23]
A. { Isn't this a beautiful _____?!
{ Aren't these beautiful _____?!
B. It's/They're magnificent.

[24–28] A. Do you worry about the environment?
B. Yes. I'm very concerned about _____.

Describe some places of natural beauty in your country.

What kind of energy do you use to heat your home? to cook?
In your opinion, which kind of energy is best for producing electricity?

ФЕРМА И ЖИВОТНЫЕ, ЖИВУЩИЕ НА ФЕРМЕ

фермерский дом	**1.** farmhouse	поле	**13.** field	цыплёнок	**26.** chick
огород	**2.** (vegetable) garden	комбайн	**14.** combine	индюк	**27.** turkey
пугало	**3.** scarecrow	луг	**15.** pasture	козёл	**28.** goat
посевы	**4.** crop	фруктовый сад	**16.** orchard	козлёнок	**29.** kid
оросительная	**5.** irrigation system	фруктовое дерево	**17.** fruit tree	овца	**30.** sheep
система		фермер	**18.** farmer	ягнёнок	**31.** lamb
амбар/сарай	**6.** barn	работник на ферме	**19.** hired hand	бык	**32.** bull
силосная башня	**7.** silo	курятник	**20.** chicken coop	молочная корова	**33.** (dairy) cow
конюшня	**8.** stable	курятник	**21.** hen house	телёнок-телята	**34.** calf–calves
сено	**9.** hay	изгородь	**22.** fence	лошадь	**35.** horse
вилы для сена	**10.** pitchfork	трактор	**23.** tractor	свинья	**36.** pig
загон около	**11.** barnyard	петух	**24.** rooster	поросёнок	**37.** piglet
амбара/сарая		курица	**25.** chicken/hen		
свинарник	**12.** pig pen/pig sty				

A. Where's the _____?
B. In/On/Next to the _____.

A. The _[24–37]_ s got loose again!
B. Oh, no! Where are they?
A. They're in the _[1, 2, 12, 13, 15, 16, 20, 21]_ !

Tell about farms in your country.
What crops and animals are common on these farms?

ДИКИЕ И ДОМАШНИЕ ЖИВОТНЫЕ

лиса	**1.** fox	бобёр	**14.** beaver	леопард	**27.** leopard
дикообраз	**2.** porcupine	летучая мышь	**15.** bat	пятна	**a.** spots
игла	**a.** quill	скунс	**16.** skunk	жираф	**28.** giraffe
енот	**3.** raccoon	опоссум	**17.** possum	бизон	**29.** bison
волк–волки	**4.** wolf–wolves	осёл	**18.** donkey	слон	**30.** elephant
лось	**5.** moose	буйвол	**19.** buffalo	бивень	**a.** tusk
рог	**a.** antler	верблюд	**20.** camel	хобот	**b.** trunk
олень	**6.** deer	горб	**a.** hump	тигр	**31.** tiger
копыто	**a.** hoof	лама	**21.** llama	лапа	**a.** paw
оленёнок	**7.** fawn	лошадь	**22.** horse	лев	**32.** lion
мышь–мыши	**8.** mouse–mice	хвост	**a.** tail	грива	**a.** mane
бурундук	**9.** chipmunk	жеребёнок	**23.** foal	бегемот	**33.** hippopotamus
крыса	**10.** rat	пони	**24.** pony	гиена	**34.** hyena
белка	**11.** squirrel	броненосец	**25.** armadillo	носорог	**35.** rhinoceros
кролик	**12.** rabbit	кенгуру	**26.** kangaroo	рог	**a.** horn
колумбийский	**13.** gopher	сумка	**a.** pouch	зебра	**36.** zebra
суслик				полосы	**a.** stripes

бурый медведь	**37.** black bear	гиббон	**44.** gibbon	Домашние животные		**Pets**
коготь	**a.** claw	бабуин	**45.** baboon	кошка	**51.** cat
гризли/гималайский	**38.** grizzly bear	орангутанг	**46.** orangutan	усы	**a.** whiskers
медведь		горилла	**47.** gorilla	котёнок	**52.** kitten
белый медведь	**39.** polar bear	муравьед	**48.** anteater	собака	**53.** dog
коала	**40.** koala (bear)	червь	**49.** worm	щенок	**54.** puppy
панда	**41.** panda	слизняк	**50.** slug	хомяк	**55.** hamster
обезьяна	**42.** monkey			песчанка	**56.** gerbil
шимпанзе	**43.** chimpanzee			морская свинка	**57.** guinea pig

[1–50] A. Look at that _____!
B. Wow! That's the biggest _____ I've ever seen!

[51–57] A. Do you have a pet?
B. Yes. I have a _____.
A. What's your _____'s name?
B. ....

What animals can be found where you live?
Is there a zoo near where you live? What animals does the zoo have?
What are some common pets in your country?

If you were an animal, which animal do you think you would be? Why?
Does your culture have any popular folk tales or children's stories about animals? Tell a story you are familiar with.

ПТИЦЫ И НАСЕКОМЫЕ

Птицы	**A. Birds**	голубь	**11.** pigeon	аист	**25.** stork	оса	**39.** wasp
малиновка	**1.** robin	сова	**12.** owl	пеликан	**26.** pelican	клещ	**40.** tick
гнездо	**a.** nest	ястреб	**13.** hawk	павлин	**27.** peacock	пчела	**41.** bee
яйцо	**b.** egg	орёл	**14.** eagle	пингвин	**28.** penguin	улей	**a.** beehive
голубая сойка	**2.** blue jay	коготь	**a.** claw	роудраннер	**29.** roadrunner	гусеница	**42.** caterpillar
крыло	**a.** wing	канарейка	**15.** canary	страус	**30.** ostrich	кокон	**a.** cocoon
хвост	**b.** tail	какаду	**16.** cockatoo			бабочка	**43.** butterfly
перо	**c.** feather	попугаи	**17.** parrot	Насекомые	**B. Insects**	кузнечик	**44.** grasshopper
кардинал	**3.** cardinal	длиннохвостий	**18.** parakeet	муха	**31.** fly	муравей	**45.** ant
колибри	**4.** hummingbird	попугаи		комар	**32.** mosquito	жук	**46.** beetle
фазан	**5.** pheasant	утка	**19.** duck	блоха	**33.** flea	термит	**47.** termite
ворона	**6.** crow	клюв	**a.** bill	светлячок	**34.** firefly/	таракан	**48.** roach/
чайка	**7.** seagull	утёнок	**20.** duckling		lightning bug		cockroach
воробей	**8.** sparrow	гусь	**21.** goose	мотылёк	**35.** moth	скорпион	**49.** scorpion
дятел	**9.** woodpecker	лебедь	**22.** swan	стрекоза	**36.** dragonfly	многоножка	**50.** centipede
клюв	**a.** beak	фламинго	**23.** flamingo	паук	**37.** spider	богомол	**51.** praying mantis
ласточка	**10.** swallow	журавль	**24.** crane	паутина	**a.** web	сверчок	**52.** cricket
				божья коровка	**38.** ladybug		

[1–52] A. Is that a/an _____?
         B. No. I think it's a/an _____.

[31–52] A. Hold still! There's a _____ on your shirt!
          B. Oh! Can you get it off of me?
          A. There! It's gone!

What birds and insects can be found where you live?

Does your culture have any popular folk tales or children's stories about birds or insects? Tell a story you are familiar with.

РЫБА, МОРСКИЕ ЖИВОТНЫЕ И РЕПТИЛИИ

Рыба	**A. Fish**
форель	**1.** trout
плавник	**a.** fin
жабры	**b.** gill
хвост	**c.** tail
морской окунь	**2.** bass
лосось	**3.** salmon
акула	**4.** shark
камбала	**5.** flounder
меч-рыба	**6.** swordfish
угорь	**7.** eel
морской конь	**8.** sea horse

Морские Животные	**B. Sea Animals**
кит	**9.** whale
дельфин	**10.** dolphin
тюлень/морской котик	**11.** seal
ласт	**a.** flipper

медуза	**12.** jellyfish
выдра	**13.** otter
морж	**14.** walrus
клык	**a.** tusk
омар/морской рак	**15.** lobster
	a. claw
краб	**16.** crab
осьминог	**17.** octopus
щупальце	**a.** tentacle
креветка	**18.** shrimp
мидия	**19.** mussel
мидия	**20.** clam
гребешок	**21.** scallop
устрица	**22.** oyster
улитка	**23.** snail
морская звезда	**24.** starfish
кальмар	**25.** squid

Земноводные животные и рептилии	**C. Amphibians and Reptiles**
черепаха	**26.** tortoise
панцырь	**a.** shell
черепаха	**27.** turtle
аллигатор	**28.** alligator
крокодил	**29.** crocodile
ящерица	**30.** lizard
игуана	**31.** iguana
головастик	**32.** tadpole
лягушка	**33.** frog
саламандра	**34.** salamander
змея	**35.** snake
гремучая змея	**36.** rattlesnake
кобра	**37.** cobra
удав	**38.** boa constrictor

[1–38] A. Is that a/an _____?
B. No. I think it's a/an _____.

[26–38] A. Are there any _____s around here?
B. No. But there are lots of _____s.

What fish, sea animals, and reptiles can be found in your country? Which ones are endangered and need to be protected? Why?

In your opinion, which ones are the most interesting? the most beautiful? the most dangerous?

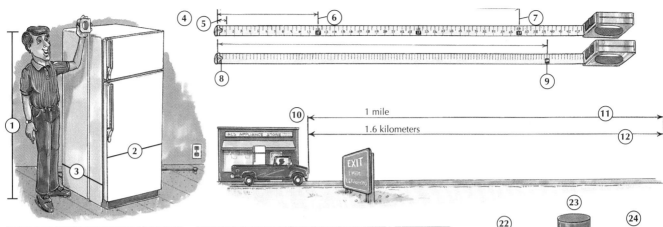

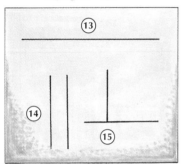

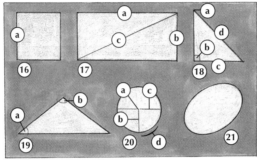

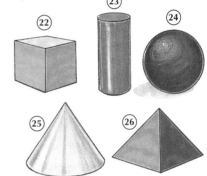

Меры измерения	**A. Measurements**	параллельные линии	**14.** parallel lines	равнобедренный	**19.** isosceles triangle
высота	**1.** height	перпендикулярные линии	**15.** perpendicular lines	треугольн	
ширина	**2.** width			острый угол	**a.** acute angle
глубина	**3.** depth	Геометрические формы	**C. Geometric Shapes**	тупой угол	**b.** obtuse angle
длина	**4.** length	квадрат	**16.** square	круг	**20.** circle
дюйм	**5.** inch	сторона	**a.** side	центр	**a.** center
фут – футы	**6.** foot–feet	прямоугольник	**17.** rectangle	радиус	**b.** radius
ярд	**7.** yard	длина	**a.** length	диаметр	**c.** diameter
сантиметр	**8.** centimeter	ширина	**b.** width	окружность	**d.** circumference
метр	**9.** meter	диагональ	**c.** diagonal	эллипс/овал	**21.** ellipse/oval
дистанция/растояние	**10.** distance	прямоугольный	**18.** right triangle		
миля	**11.** mile	треугольник		Геометрические	**D. Solid Figures**
километр	**12.** kilometer	вершина	**a.** apex	фигуры	
		прямой угол	**b.** right angle	куб	**22.** cube
Линии	**B. Lines**	основание	**c.** base	цилиндр	**23.** cylinder
прямая линия	**13.** straight line	гипотенуза	**d.** hypotenuse	шар	**24.** sphere
				конус	**25.** cone
				пирамида	**26.** pyramid

1 inch (1")	=	2.54 centimeters (cm)
1 foot (1')	=	0.305 meters (m)
1 yard (1 yd.)	=	0.914 meters (m)
1 mile (mi.)	=	1.6 kilometers (km)

[1–9]
A. What's the ___[1–4]___ ?
B. .... ___[5–9]___ (s).

[11–12]
A. What's the distance?
B. .... _____ (s).

[16–21]
A. Who can tell me what shape this is?
B. I can. It's a/an _____.

[22–26]
A. Who knows what figure this is?
B. I do. It's a/an _____.

[13–26]
A. This painting is magnificent!
B. Hmm. I don't think so. It just looks like a lot of _____s and _____s to me!

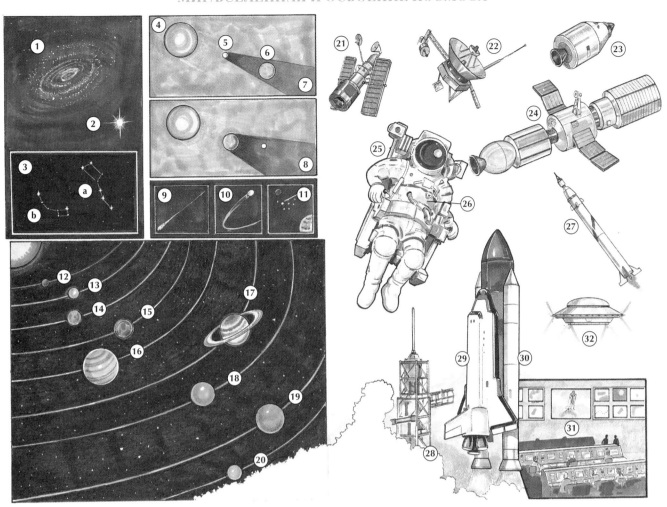

Мир/Вселенная	**A. The Universe**	комета	**10.** comet	спутник Земли	**23.** space craft/orbiter
галактика	**1.** galaxy	астероид	**11.** asteroid	космическая станция	**24.** space station
звезда	**2.** star	Меркурий	**12.** Mercury	космонавт	**25.** astronaut
созвездие	**3.** constellation	Венера	**13.** Venus	космический костюм	**26.** space suit
Большая Медведица	**a.** The Big Dipper	Земля	**14.** Earth	ракета	**27.** rocket
Малая Медведица	**b.** The Little Dipper	Марс	**15.** Mars	стартовая площадка	**28.** launch pad
		Юпитер	**16.** Jupiter	космический корабль	**29.** space shuttle
Солнечная Система	**B. The Solar System**	Сатурн	**17.** Saturn	ракетный ускоритель	**30.** booster rocket
солнце	**4.** sun	Уран	**18.** Uranus	пункт контроля	**31.** mission control
луна	**5.** moon	Нептун	**19.** Neptune	за полётом	
планета	**6.** planet	Плутон	**20.** Pluto	летающая	**32.** U.F.O./ Unidentified/
солнечное затмение	**7.** solar eclipse			тарелка/НЛО	Flying Object/
лунное затмение	**8.** lunar eclipse	Освоение космоса	**C. Space Exploration**		flying saucer
метеор	**9.** meteor	спутник	**21.** satellite		
		зонд	**22.** (space) probe		

[1–20]

A. Is that (a/an/the) _____?

B. I'm not sure. I think it might be (a/an/the) _____.

[21–27, 29, 31]

A. Is the _____ ready for tomorrow's launch?

B. Yes. "All systems are go!"

Pretend you are an astronaut traveling in space.
   What do you see?
Draw and name a constellation you are familiar with.

Do you think space exploration is important? Why?
Have you ever seen a U.F.O.? Do you believe there is
   life in outer space? Why?

ГЛОССАРИЙ

абажур **14**-7
абрикос **44**-6
аварийный выход **97**-23
аварийный тормоз **93**-68
авиа **75**-6
авиаписьмо **75**-3
авокадо **44**-13
Австралия **6**-7
автобус **38**-15, **95**-18
автобусная остановка **34**-7, **38**-12, **95**-23
автовокзал **95**-21
автомат **90**-19, **95**-31
автомат по продаже марок **75**-28
автомат по продаже проездных билетов **95**-35
автомат с газированной водой **86**-25
автоматическая трансмиссия **93**-72
автоматический кассовый аппарат **67**-17
автомобиль **92**
автомобиль с откидным верхом **93**-87
автомобиль со спичечную коробку **65**-16
автоответчик **64**-14
автор **76**-27
автосиденье **20**-21
автостоянка **26**-18, **36**-14, **62**-20
агент бюро путешествий **83**-25
агент по продаже билетов **96**-2
агент по продаже домов **82**-11
агентство путешествий **37**-27
адаптер **64**-29
адрес **1**-5, **75**-19
Азия **6**-6
аист **118**-25
акваланг **107**-18
аккордеон **112**-32
аккредитивы **67**-5
аккумулятор **92**-33
аккуратный **40**-41
акселератор **93**-70
актёр **80**-2, **110**-9
актриса **80**-3, **110**-8
акула **119**-4
акустическая гитара **112**-5
акушер **72**-8
алгебра **78**-2
аллигатор **119**-28
альбом для марок **109**-19
альбом для монет **109**-21
альт **112**-2

алюминевая фольга **49**-61
амбар **115**-6
американский сыр **48**-7
американский футбол **79**-26, **104**-C
аммиачный раствор **24**-25
амфитеатр **110**-15
анализ крови **73**-15
анализы **73**-14
ананас **44**-16
ананасовый сок **46**-27
английская флейта **112**-15
английские булочки **47**-70
английский язык **78**-6
Антарктика **6**-8
антенна **92**-11
антикислотные таблетки **74**-7
антипасто **55**-10
анютины глазки **113**-36
апельсин **44**-21
апельсиновый сок **46**-6
аптека **35**-22
аптекарь **82**-6
аптечка **22**-19
аптечка скорой помощи **90**-14
арахис **48**-23
арахисовая паста **49**-49
арбуз **44**-17
арендная плата **27**-19
арифметика **31**
арифмометр **64**-27, **87**-9
артерии **69**-79
артишок **45**-24
арфа **112**-10
архитектор **80**-4
аспирин **74**-1
ассистент **76**-3, **86**-32
астероид **121**-11
астрономия **109**-Q
атлас **76**-13
афиша **110**-32
Африка **6**-4
аэровокзал **97**-33
аэросани **106**-12
аэропорт **96**

бабочка **118**-43
бабуин **117**-45
бабушка **2**-10
багаж **95**-11, **96**-21
багажная карусель **96**-17
багажная тележка **96**-19
багажник **92**-13, 16
багажный номерок **96**-23
байдарка **107**-7
баки **68**-24
баклажан **45**-9

балерина **110**-28
балеро **110**-27
балет **110**-D
балетная труппа **110**-29
балетные тапочки **110**-30, 31
балка **91**-32
балкон **26**-19, **110**-16
баллон с ядохимикатом **29**-31
бампер **92**-2
банан **44**-4
банджо **112**-24
банк **34**-4, 67
банджо **112**-8
банка **50**-12
банковская книжка **67**-4
банковский сейф **67**-13
барабан **112**-22
баранка **54**-3
бараньи отбивные **47**-50
баранья нога **47**-49
барьер **94**-8, 13
баскетбол **104**-F
баскетболист **104**-11
баскетбольная корзина **105**-23
баскетбольная площадка **104**-12
баскетбольные кроссовки **58**-29
баскетбольный мяч **105**-21
баскетбольный щит **105**-22
бассейн **26**-20
батат **45**-26, 27
батут **103**-45
батарейки **29**-25
бег **102**-B
бег трусцой **102**-A
бегать **108**-14
бегемот **116**-33
беговая дорожка **77**-16, **100**-1
беговой костюм **59**-8
беговые кроссовки **59**-28, **102**-2, 4
беговые шорты **59**-5, **102**-3
бедный **40**-50
бедро **68**-36, 39
бежевый **56**-12
безымянный палец **69**-48
бейсбол **104**-A
бейсболист **104**-1
бейсбольная форма **105**-4
бейсбольная шапочка **59**-29
бейсбольное поле **104**-2
бейсбольные перчатки **105**-6
бейсбольный мяч **105**-1
бекон **47**-56
белая доска **86**-22
белка **116**-11

белый **56**-9
белый медведь **117**-39
белый хлеб **54**-29
бельевая верёвка **24**-38
бельевая корзина **24**-30
бельевая прищепка **24**-39
бензобак **92**-24
бензоколонка **35**-25, **92**-39, 44
бензоуказатель **93**-49
берет **59**-30
берёза **113**-17
беспошлинный магазин **96**-15
библиотека **36**-5, 76
библиотекарь **76**-1
библиотечная карточка **76**-30
бивень **116**-30a
бизнес-карточки **88**-20
бизон **116**-29
билет **96**-3, **110**-19
билет для пересадки **95**-27
билетёр **110**-17
билетная касса **95**-22, **96**-1, **110**-33
билетное окошко **95**-2
биллиард **103**-R
биллиардные шары **103**-37
биллиардный стол **103**-36
бинокль **109**-25
биология **78**-10
бисквит **54**-6
бита **105**-2
бить мяч об пол **108**-8
бифштекс **47**-47
бланк для регистрации воинской повинности **75**-17
бланк "Смена адреса" **75**-16
блейзер **57**-23
блестящий **41**-65
Ближний Восток **6**-5
блокнот **89**-12
блокнот для телефонных звонков **89**-14
блокнот с клейкими листами **89**-13
блоха **118**-33
блуграсс **111**-10
блуза **57**-7
блюдце **16**-8
блюз **111**-9
бобёр **116**-14
бобслей **106**-11
богатый **40**-49
богомол **118**-51
божья коровка **118**-38
бокал **16**-6
боковая дверь **25**-25
бокс **103**-W

доска с зажимом **88**-21
доска с колёсами **102**-10
Достань *лист бумаги.* **11**-21
достать руками **108**-21
дочь **2**-5
драма **79**-25, **111**-13, 16, 24
дренажная труба **25**-20
дробь **31**
дротики **103**-Q, 35
дуб **113**-19
дупло **70**-18
дуршлаг **19**-10
духи **23**-29
духовка **18**-21
духовые инструменты **112**
душ **22**-32
душевая шапочка **23**-8
душевой занавес **22**-36
душевой кран **22**-34
дымодетектор **26**-7
дымоход **25**-15
дыхательное горло **69**-64
дюжина **50**-9
дюйм **120**-5
дюна **114**-18
дядя **3**-2
дятел **118**-9

евангелистская музыка **111**-7
Европа **6**-3
еда **97**-27
енот **116**-3

жабры **119**-1b
жакет **57**-22, **59**-14
жар **70**-7
жареная курица **54**-14
жареная рыба **55**-17
жарить **53**-8, 19
жарить на вертеле **53**-23
жаркий **98**-21
(ему) жарко **42**-4
жаркое **47**-46
жаровня **19**-7
жаровня без крышки **19**-6
жевательная резинка **49**-87
желе **49**-47, **55**-28
железнодорожный переход
 94-25
желудок **69**-70
жемчужное ожерелье **60**-6
жемчужный лук **45**-34
жена **2**-1
женатый **40**-47
женский туалет **62**-8
женщина, проверяющая
 счётчики **38**-18
жеребёнок **116**-23
жестяная коробка **18**-18
жёлтый **56**-4
жёлтый нарцисс **113**-32
жёлчный пузырь **69**-69
живот **68**-30

животные, живущие
 на ферме **115**
жидкие витамины **21**-12
жидкое моющее средство **18**-3
жидкое мыло **49**-60
жидкость для исправления
 ошибок **89**-33
жидкость для полоскания
 рта **23**-22
жилет **57**-26
жираф **116**-28
жирный **40**-23
жук **118**-46
журавль **118**-24
журнал **49**-86, **76**-23
журнал (научный) **76**-24
журналист **81**-30

завистливый **43**-31
завод **90**
завтракать **8**-19
завуч **77**-18
загон около амбара **115**-11
загон около сарая **115**-11
загорающий **101**-11
загрязнение воздуха **114**-24, 28
заднее стекло **92**-14
задний дефростер **92**-15
задняя дверь **25**-22
задняя фара **92**-17
зажигание **93**-61
зажим **89**-6
заказная почта **75**-9
заколка **60**-9
заколки для волос **23**-15
Закрой *свою книгу.* **11**-9
закрытый **41**-58
закуски **48**-В, **55**-А
закусочный бар **62**-18, **101**-4
зал заседаний **86**-20
зал ожидания **96**-12
зал получения багажа **96**-16
залив **114**-21
заложило нос **71**-31
замок **26**-10
замок из песка **101**-12
замороженные овощи **47**-76
замороженные продукты **47**-J
замороженные ужины **47**-77
замороженный апельсиновый
 сок **47**-79
замороженный лимонад **47**-78
замужний **40**-47
занавес **110**-2
заниматься **9**-19
занятие спортом **103**-Y
запад **5**-4
запасное колесо **92**-26
запечёная курица **55**-16
Записывай. **11**-30
запонки **60**-12
запястье **69**-44
зарплата, выданная чеком
 88-25

зарубежный фильм **111**-20
застелить постель **8**-11
защитные очки **90**-4
заявление о займе **67**-12
звезда **121**-2
звонок **26**-3
звуковая кассета **63**-17
здание суда **38**-4
здоровье **78**-16
зебра **116**-36
зелёная фасоль **45**-14
зелёный **56**-5
зелёный боб **45**-15
зелёный лук **45**-32
зелёный перец **45**-28
Земля **121**-14
земляные орехи **48**-23
земноводные животные **119**-С
зеркало **17**-18, **22**-18
зеркало бокового вида **92**-10
зеркало заднего вида **93**-47
зерновые хлопья **46**-19
зима **98**-28
змея **119**-35
знак ограничения скорости
 94-20
золовка **3**-12
золотой **56**-20
зонд **121**-22
зонт **60**-25
зоомагазин **36**-15
зоопарк **37**-30, **100**-10
зрачок **68**-11
зрители **110**-12
зрительный зал **77**-13
зуб **68**-21
зубило **28**-12
зубная боль **70**-3
зубная паста **23**-21
зубная щётка **22**-24, **23**-1
зубной врач **72**-6
зубное кольцо **21**-17
зудящий **71**-50
зукини **45**-10
зять **3**-9

игла **113**-9, **116**-2а
игра в кегли **102**-G
игра в стеклянные шарики
 109-36
играть **9**-15, **84**-1
играть в баскетбол **9**-16
играть во фризби **103**-P
играть на гитаре **9**-17
играть на *рояле* **85**-18
игровая площадка **100**-18
игровое шоу **111**-27
игрушка **20**-17, **65**-15
игры **109**-R
игуана **119**-31
идёт град **98**-11
идёт дождь **98**-8
идёт снег **98**-10
Иди к *доске.* **11**-2

изгородь **115**-22
изготовитель воздушной
 кукурузы **19**-28
изготовитель льда **18**-29
измерительная линейка **29**-23
измерительная ложка **19**-18
измерительная чашка **19**-17
измученный **71**-32
изнурённый **42**-3, **71**-32
изобразительное искусство
 78-20
изогнутый **40**-18
изолента **29**-28
Изучай *восьмую страницу.*
 11-8
изюм **44**-27
изящный **61**-9
икота **70**-20
икра **68**-41
иммиграционная служба **96**-27
имя **1**-1, 2
инвалидная коляска **74**-15
индексная карточка **89**-11
индюк **115**-27
индюшатина **48**-5
индюшка **47**-43
инжир **44**-11
инфекция **70**-11
информационная будка **95**-4
информационный отдел **76**-16
информация **76**-9
испанский язык **78**-13
Исправь *свои ошибки.* **11**-19
испуганный **43**-26
испытывающий жажду **42**-7
история **78**-7

йогурт **46**-13

кабачок **45**-11, 12
кабина **97**-1
кабинет **77**-1, **86**-13
кабинет советника **77**-3
кадка **51**-19
какаду **118**-16
какао **48**-42
кактус **113**-47
калькулятор **10**-15, **64**-26, **87**-8
кальмар **119**-25
камбала **119**-5
каменщик **80**-10
камера **101**-23
камень **101**, **109**-16
камин **14**-24
каминная полка **14**-23
каминный экран **14**-25
камзол **58**-14
канарейка **118**-15
канделябр **15**-5
канистра **29**-2
каноэ **107**-3
канцелярия **77**-1, **86**
канцелярская скрепка **89**-1
канцелярские товары **89**

скунс 116-16
скучающий 43-27
слесарь 27-7
слива 44-5
слизняк 117-50
словарь 76-15
сложение 31
сломать 71-46
слон 116-30
служба безопасности 96-В
Слушай *вопрос.* 11-11
слушать музыку 9-13
слушать радио 9-12
смеситель 19-29
сметана 46-10
смешать... с ... 53-15
смешивать... с ... 53-14
смокинг 57-29
смотреть телевизор 9-11
Смотри *кино.* 11-29
смущённый 43-29
смягчитель 24-19
снабженец 83-20
снежный буран 98-16
снимать кожу 53-5
сноха 3-10
собака 117-53
Собери *тесты* .11-25
сова 118-12
советник 77-20
совок 24-2, 29-10
согнуться 108-12
соевый соус 48-32
созвездие 121-3
сок 46-D
сок в пакетиках 46-33
сок в порошке 46-34
солёные огурцы 48-27
солнечная система 121-В
солнечная энергия 114-34
солнечное затмение 121-7
солнечные очки 101-26
солнечный 98-1
солнечный ожог 70-14
солнце 121-4
соломинки 49-55
солонина 48-6
солонка 15-15
соль 48-29
сонливый 42-2
сосиска 54-10
сосиски 47-54
соска 21-13, 15
сосна 113-20
сопеть 71-35
сопло 92-45
Сотри *своё имя.* 11-4
софтбол 104-В
софтболист 104-3
софтбольная перчатка 105-9
софтбольный мяч 105-8
спагетти 46-22
спагетти с фрикадельками 55-18

спазмы 70-22
спальный вагон 95-16
спальный мешок 99-3
спаржа 45-8
спасатель 101-1
спасательная будка 101-2
спасательный жилет 97-31, 107-2, 10
спасательный круг 101-3
спать 8-15
специальность 80
специи 48-31
спидометр 93-51
спина 68-31
спинка 17-2, 12
спинной мозг 69-65
спирт 72-26
сплошная линия 94-19
спортивная машина 93-86
спортивная программа 111-29
спортивная рубашка 57-4
спортивное снаряжение 105
справочник 62-1, 109-26
справочный отдел 76-12
спутник 121-21
спутник Земли 121-23
средний палец 69-47
средний ряд 94-15
стабилизатор 64-28
ставень 25-12
стакан 22-23
стакан для воды 16-5
стакан для карандашей 88-4
стаместка 28-12
станция метро 38-20, 95-28
станция техобслуживания 92-41
стартовая площадка 121-28
старый 40-28, 30
статуя/памятник 100-3
ствол 113-6
стебель 113-27
стегание 109-G
стена 14-13
стенка 14-14
стереосистема 14-17, 63-13
стетоскоп 72-19
стёганое одеяло 17-11
стиральная машина 24-16
стиральный порошок 24-18
стирать 9-6
стирательная резинка 10-7, 88-36
стоимость проезда 95-25
стойка на руках 108-36
сток 22-37
стол 15-1, 88-1
стол для пикника 100-5
стол регистрации 96-9
стол регистрации книг 76-2
столик 14-5, 97-26
столик для пеленания 20-9
столик у кровати 73-24
столовая 77-4, 90-22

столовая ложка 74-21
стоп 94-38
сторож 83-19
сторона 120-16а
сточная труба 39-25
стоянка такси 39-22, 95-36
стоянка-гараж 26-17, 36-13, 62-10
стояночный счётчик 38-17
страна 12
страус 118-30
страховочный пояс 99-13
стрекоза 118-36
стрела 91-17
стрельба из лука 103-V
стрелять 108-28
стремена 102-16
стремянка 29-21
строитель 81-17
строительные леса 91-13
строительный учаток 91
строить 84-4
струнные инструменты 112-А
студенческое самоуправление 79-30
стул 10-4, 15-2
стул для газона 25-30
ступня 69-53
стюардесса 97-9
сувенирный магазин 96-14
судно 73-25
сук 113-5
сумак 113-50
сумка 60-21, 116-26а
сумка для книг 60-22
сумка для фотоаппарата 64-18
сумочка 60-20
суп 46-15
супермаркет 37-23
супная тарелка 16-4
суспензорий 58-9
сустав 69-52
сухое печенье 46-21
сухой 41-56
сушилка 24-17
сцена 110-5
сцепление 93-73
счастливый 42-10
счетовод 80-9
счёт за воду 27-15
счёт за газ 27-12
счёт за дезинфекцию 27-18
счёт за кабельное телевидение 27-17
счёт за телефон 27-14
счёт за тепло 27-16
счёт за электричество 27-13
счётчик 95-38
съезд (знак) 94-22
сын 2-6
сыр 46-7
сыр "моццарелла" 48-10
сыпь 70-12
севн-ап 54-15

таблетка 74-17
таблетки от горла 74-6
таблетки от простуды 74-2
таблица (глазная) 72-16
табличка с именем 88-9
табло прибытия и отправления 95-3
такси 38-13, 95-37
таксист 38-14, 83-22, 95-40
талия 68-35
таможенная декларация 96-26
таможенник 96-25
таможня 96-24
танцор 110-7
тапочки 58-5
таракан 118-48
тарелка для катания с горы 106-10
тарелка для салата 16-1
тарелка для ужина 16-3
тарелка для хлеба и масла 16-2
тарелка супа "чили" 54-13
тарелки 112-26
тачка 29-6, 91-1
твёрдый 40-36
театр 37-24, 110-А
телевизионная антенна 25-14
телевизионные программы 111-D
телевизионщик 27-6
телевизор 10-30, 14-15, 63-1
тележка 65-30, 90-24
тележка для покупок 49-72
телекс 87-14
телескоп 109-28
телефон 64-12, 87-11
телефонная будка 39-23
телефонная система 87-13
телёнок 115-34
тело 68
телячья котлета 55-15
температура 70-7
тема 76-29
температура 98-В
тени 23-36
теннис 102-К
теннисная ракетка 102-20
теннисные кроссовки 58-27
теннисные шорты 59-6
теннисный мяч 102-21, 32
теннисный стол 102-30
теплоизоляция 91-28
тереть 53-4
терраса 26-19
термит 118-47
термометр 93-50, 98-18
термос 99-15
тесный 40-14
тесть 3-8
тетрадь 10-11, 89-15
техник, делающий рентограммы 72-3

GLOSSARY

The bold number indicates the page(s) on which the word appears; the number that follows indicates the word's location in the illustration and in the word list on the page. For example, "north **5**-1" indicates that the word *north* is on page 5 and is item number 1.

white **56**-9
white bread **54**-29
white water rafting **107**-E
whiteboard **86**-22
whole wheat bread **54**-31
wide **40**-21, **61**-15
width **120**-2,17b
wife **2**-1
willow **113**-22
wind **114**-32
windbreaker **59**-15
window **14**-8, **25**-10, **75**-25
window cleaner **24**-24
window screen **25**-11
window seat **97**-16
windpipe **69**-64
windshield **92**-8
windshield wipers **92**-9
windsurfing **107**-J
windy **98**-6
wine glass **16**-6
wing **97**-40, **118**-2a
winter **98**-28
wipes **21**-7, **49**-67
wire **28**-27, **91**-27
withdrawal slip **67**-9
wok **19**-1
wolf **116**-4
Women's Clothing Department
    62-11
wood **91**-25
woodpecker **118**-9
woods **114**-1
woodwind **112**-B
woodworking **109**-K
word processor **87**-6
work **11**-14
work boots **58**-33
work gloves **29**-13
work out **103**-Y
work station **86**-9, **90**-8
worker **90**-7
worm **117**-49
worried **43**-25
wrench **28**-4
wrestle **103**-X
wrestling mat **103**-53
wrestling uniform **103**-52
wrist **69**-44
wrist watch **60**-10
write **11**-3, **85**-28

X-ray machine **72**-18, **96**-7
X-ray technician **72**-3
X-rays **73**-13
xylophone **112**-27

yam **45**-27
yard **120**-7
yardstick **29**-23
yarn **109**-9
year **33**
yearbook **79**-28
yellow **56**-4

yield sign **94**-23
yogurt **46**-13
young **40**-29

zebra **116**-36
zip code **1**-11, **75**-20
zoo **37**-30, **100**-10
zoom lens **64**-17
zucchini (squash) **45**-10